when a
woman
loves *a man*

when a **woman loves** *a man*

· ·

Pursuing His Heart

JAMES FORD JR.

MOODY PUBLISHERS
CHICAGO

All Scripture quotations, unless otherwise indicated, are taken from the *New American Standard Bible*, Copyright © 1960, 1962, 1963, 1968, 1971, 1972, 1973, 1975, 1977, 1996 by the Lockman Foundation. Used by permission. (www.Lockman.org)

Scripture quotations marked KJV are taken from the King James Version.

Edited by Kathryn Hall
Interior design: Ragont Design
Cover design: Brand Navigation LLC
Cover images: iStockphoto.com

Library of Congress Cataloging-in-Publication Data

Ford, James, 1951-
When a woman loves a man / James Ford, Jr.
    p. cm.
 ISBN 978-0-8024-6837-6
1. Wives--Religious life. 2. Christian women--Religious life. 3.
Marriage--Religious aspects--Christianity. I. Title.

 BV4528.15.F67 2011
 248.8'435--dc22

2010047808

3 5 7 9 10 8 6 4

Printed in the United States of America

I thank my Lord Jesus Christ for His "so great salvation" that saved me in time and for eternity. I dedicate this book to my "Sugarbabe," Leslie Ann Ford, who loves herself some James Ford Jr. You have kept all the original poetry I've written for you, so here's another one for your collection.

I was arrested and place in custody by your Christ-like character and pleasant personality. They locked me up and placed me in the prison of your love. The governor wanted to grant me a pardon so I could get an early release. But I turned it down. The parole board gave me permission to get an early release, but I told them that loving you is a life sentence and I want to do all my time. I don't want a pardon and I don't want an early release because I am forever a prisoner of your love.

Contents

Introduction—9

Introduction

A WOMAN OF VIRTUE. A wise man once asked, "Who can find her?" Well, under the inspiration of the Holy Spirit, that same man gave the definitive description of a woman in pursuit of excellence. This man was King Solomon and he wrote the book of Proverbs thousands of years ago. Yet, following his narrative even today will lead anyone who knows her to discover a woman who conducts her life in an admirable, upright, and godly fashion.

Let me frame the context of the pages of this book. We are in search of this particular kind of woman. The Word of God calls her a virtuous woman because she excels in all her ways. Furthermore, if or when she marries, the virtuous woman will naturally become an excellent wife. When people look at her, they will have no other recourse than to be inspired because they will see a reflection of the divine model that God created all women to be.

I feel it is important that the message be presented concerning the virtuous woman found in Proverbs, chapter 31. In fact, it is so vital to the very foundation of the Christian marriage that it will be the focal point throughout this book. With the help of biblical examples of virtuous women who reflect God's divine design, the description of such a righteous person will be conveyed in practical terms and through the fundamental ways in which a woman loves a man.

To begin the process, allow me to turn your attention to the book of Proverbs. King Solomon took off his crown and put on his preacher's robe, and then he wrote:

"The fear of the Lord is the beginning of knowledge."
(Proverbs 1:7)

That's how he began his sermon, by setting the record straight on the value of wisdom. At its very foundation, the one who searches for wisdom will find and embrace a holy and sincere reverence for God. It is called the "fear of the Lord," and it will lead an individual to a closer understanding of God and His extraordinary ways. For, indeed, one cannot walk with God unless one knows something about Him.

I must admit that Solomon's approach was a little better than most of us preachers because we'll tell you what to do—but typically, we don't tell you how to do it.

As you study his work, you will notice that Solomon opened

up his sermon and captured the key principles all the way through the book. The message on the importance of wisdom that he began in chapter 1, ended with him giving the picture of it in chapter 31, when he wrote this magnificent passage:

An excellent wife, who can find? For her worth is far above jewels. The heart of her husband trusts in her, and he will have no lack of gain. She does him good and not evil all the days of her life. She looks for wool and flax and works with her hands in delight. She is like merchant ships; she brings her food from afar. She rises also while it is still night and gives food to her household and portions to her maidens. She considers a field and buys it; from her earnings she plants a vineyard. She girds herself with strength and makes her arms strong. She senses that her gain is good; her lamp does not go out at night. She stretches out her hands to the distaff, and her hands grasp the spindle. She extends her hand to the poor, and she stretches out her hands to the needy. She is not afraid of the snow for her household, for all her household are clothed with scarlet. She makes coverings for herself; her clothing is fine linen and purple. Her husband is known in the gates, when he sits among the elders of the land. She makes linen garments and sells them, and supplies belts to the tradesmen. Strength and dignity are her clothing, and she smiles at the future. She opens her mouth in wisdom, and the teaching of kindness is on her tongue. She looks well to the ways of her household, and does not eat the bread of idleness. Her children rise up and bless her; her husband also, and he praises her, saying: 'Many daughters have done nobly, but you excel them all.' Charm is deceitful and beauty is vain, but a woman who fears the Lord, she shall be praised. Give her the product of her hands, and let her works praise her in the gates. (Proverbs 31:10–31)

Scripture reveals a precious gem that, if applied with diligence, would prove some profoundly positive results for the woman who is conscientious about her walk with God. Because it sums up the description of this noble woman, it bears repeating. Take note of this treasure:

"Charm is deceitful and beauty is vain, but a woman who fears the Lord, she shall be praised." (Proverbs 31:30)

God has an extraordinary image of what He considers to be a perfect woman and therefore an excellent wife. Superior to all the lovely physical and mental traits a woman may possess, she can simply be identified as one who "fears the Lord."

A RIGHT RELATIONSHIP

A woman of virtue carries herself in a way that people can readily recognize her primary desire is to be focused on pleasing God. Although this woman doesn't dress in a manner that draws attention to herself, she is hard to miss. She doesn't wear big crosses or carry a Bible that requires the assistance of a forklift, but she is easily recognized as a virtuous woman. There is a godliness about her that is hard to miss. Furthermore, it isn't possible to respect the authority of other people when an individual doesn't give the Lord His due respect. That is why the virtuous woman's husband, in particular, will see a reflection of Christ in his wife.

Through God's omniscient and generous nature, He has provided everything that mankind needs to be successful in life. This is what makes the passage on the excellent wife a thing of beauty. Because of it, women have been given some godly principles to which they can aspire. The more they are practiced, the more a virtuous woman will learn how she must conduct herself in all her relationships.

First and foremost, the message is about her being rightly related to her Maker. Once she achieves that essential goal, her relationship with the Lord positions her to be rightly related to her mate. With those two primary relationships working for her, she will take an honorable approach to the management of her household. She won't need cues from the world on how to manage her household. Her husband won't become accustomed to unpleasant surprises.

Notice a pattern here? The woman who has all of this working in her favor is growing exponentially and maturing spiritually. With all aspects of her life in alignment, her career or other goals will be correctly aligned. This is a woman who is secure enough in who she is that she doesn't see prioritizing her household as taking a step back. In summary, according to Proverbs 31, the woman who fears the Lord has really got it going on.

As we delve deeper into the characteristics of a virtuous woman, you will find that the information in the chapters of this book will dovetail and interweave. This is because God created the woman in an extremely intricate and refined pattern. He has designed her with such great precision that it would serve any woman well to learn more about her design and the supplementary ability she possesses when she takes on the role of being a wife.

Along with discovering the purpose God gave her, that is, to be the complement of her husband, a woman's ability to submit to the man she loves will be made apparent. This knowledge will then be highlighted and supported by three crucial ingredients God placed within her—to cherish, care for, and cover him with her love.

For every woman who will read *When a Woman Loves a Man*, it is my sincere hope that the following discussion will motivate and inspire you to confirm to the men in your life that you indeed love them by exhibiting the characteristics and qualities of a woman crowned with virtue. After all, when a woman loves a man, she will do no less!

Chapter One

by divine design

when a woman loves *a man,*

she fulfills God's design

YOU'RE PROBABLY familiar with the old motto: A woman's place is in the home. Well, in today's society that idea has changed drastically. I know some women are saying, "Thank God things have changed." As a matter of fact, the change has been so dramatic that I actually saw a bumper sticker that read: A woman's place is in the mall.

With the prevalence of this postmodern mind-set, a woman's world has been transformed exponentially. But you may be surprised that a few women believe it has expanded too much. They feel that too much is expected of women and wives today. Someone once said, "They expect us to look like a girl, dress like a boy, think like a man, and work like a horse."

However, when you stop and consider what the Word of God has to say about the woman's role in marriage, there is a good deal of truth revealed in that comment. That's why, if you want to know the real truth about anything, you have to go back to its source. In this case, I'm referring to the Word of God. It contains the Divine Design, the blueprint of God's plan for all of creation.

A PERFECT WIFE?

When a woman loves a man, God has equipped her to give that man something he can feel—physically and spiritually. As I was thinking about the concept of what makes a good wife, I asked myself the question: What would the average man consider to be the attributes of a perfect wife? No doubt most men would agree with my answer.

The perfect woman looks like Halle Berry, has a body like Tyra Banks, keeps house like Martha Stewart, cooks like Paula Deen, has the mind of Mae Jemison, and possesses a fortune like Oprah Winfrey. Moreover, the perfect wife exemplifies the personality of Phylicia Rashad, the compassion of Mother Teresa, and the sex drive of Madonna. Can I get an Amen from the brothers?

When I put all of these traits together, I conclude that she needs to be a woman just like my wife.

Yet, it shouldn't be a surprise that the passage in chapter 31 of the book of Proverbs portrays a completely different picture than the amusing one described above.

Great Expectations

The truth is, everyone has expectations. Husbands have expectations for their wives as much as wives have expectations for their husbands. Sometimes those hopes are met, and sometimes they're not. Not only that, but many times the expectations are not known, so a lot of friction comes into play because of these hidden expectations.

So what does a man expect from the woman he marries? Here's one person's take on the answer:

A man wants his wife to be beautiful without ever needing to get her hair done. She doesn't like manicures and pedicures. She's always cheerful and never gets sick. Fortunately for her husband, she's allergic to jewelry and fur coats. She's an expert in keeping quiet. Her favorite pastime is taking out the garbage, and she loves to mow the lawn. She's got Einstein's brains and the body of a goddess. Lastly, and this is extremely necessary, she wants you to go out with the boys often so she can be free to sew and iron.

Well, ladies, please forgive me for that bit of levity. It's merely a little attempt at amusement and I just added it because the brothers always say that I dog them out. So I hope this makes me an equal opportunity commentator.

First Things First

Putting all humor aside, I want to begin by addressing the subject of what God anticipated when He created man and woman. After some careful consideration of God's Word, we can find out what God expects from both genders. This is important for all of us to know because He will hold every individual accountable for our actions.

So let's back up to the beginning and find out what was going on in the book of Genesis because it's time to set the record straight. Listen to this account from Genesis 2:

> "Then the Lord God took the man and put him into the garden of Eden to cultivate it and keep it. The Lord God commanded the man, saying, "From any tree of the garden you may eat freely; but from the tree of the knowledge of good and evil you shall not eat, for in the day that you eat from it you will surely die." (Genesis 2:15–17)

In this first verse we find that God put the man He created in the garden and told him to take care of it. By these actions, God gave Adam dominion and stewardship over the rest of creation. Dominion meant he was to rule well. Stewardship was to rule and take care of it. Cultivate it to keep, nurture, and do what needs to be done to ensure healthy growth. In the next two verses, God told Adam

When a Woman Loves a Man

what He expected of him. *"You may eat freely,"* God said, indicating His provisions for the man. When Adam heard this gracious invitation, worship was to be the proper response because man was created to worship the Almighty God.

This applies to all of us. We should be eternally grateful in worship to God because of His bountiful blessings. Then, the final instruction for Adam was a warning from God: "You shall not eat . . . you will surely die." Altogether, this interaction between God and man bound the two of them in a mutual relationship.

But from Adam's viewpoint, this is where the story gets real interesting. Scripture says God saw that none of His created beings were compatible with the man, and He declared, "It is not good for the man to be alone," (Genesis 2:18a). Having Adam's needs in mind, God was ready to create a suitable companion for the man, a partner with whom he could fellowship. Clearly, God wanted Adam to have someone he could connect with; someone who looked like him. I can only imagine what Adam was thinking when he opened his eyes and discovered his lovely bride—Eve, who resembled him in form but not aesthetics. Thank God! This new creation of God's thought like him, moved like him, felt like him, talked like him. In other words, God presented Adam with a creation designed specifically to complement him.

Who's in Charge?

In all of His creation work, God set definite patterns for how things should function. Adam and Eve were first, but they represent every man and woman. Through the first couple, God established the details of the relationship He envisioned for married couples. However, we have a lot more to learn about the very specific roles that God intended for us and how we are to relate with our Creator.

The apostle Paul reiterated God's plans when he laid out the divine hierarchy for our relationship with God in this way,

> "I want you to understand that Christ is the head of every man, and the man is the head of a woman, and God is the head of Christ . . . For a man ought not to have his head covered, since he is the image and glory of God; but the woman is the glory of man. For man does not originate from woman, but woman from man; for indeed man was not created for the woman's sake, but woman for the man's sake." (1 Corinthians 11:3, 7–9)

When God drew up His master plan, the blueprint for all of creation, this is the way authority was designated. According to His divine design, there is absolutely no inferiority implied between God and Christ, nor between man and woman. Following this analogy, there is equality in the respective relationships with distinction in the definition of roles.

Here is where we also find that God made Adam in His image, the *Imago Dei*. Endowed with a personality, intellect, emotion, and will, Adam became a human reflection of God's own image. He holds the distinction of being created first and was given the responsibility of being the spiritual leader in his household.

Eve was the prototype of the model woman. As the reflection of every woman, we study her to learn how she was designed to function. Since she came "out of the man," Scripture identifies her as "the glory of man." Clearly, the Master Designer established these role assignments out of His infinite love and wisdom. I believe that it causes God much pain when He watches us misuse and abuse His excellent plan.

Follow the Blueprint

So when God created marriage, what did He create it to do and to be? Sounds like a good question to me. The reality is that no one knows better than a designer what the intent of a respective design should be. For the purpose of understanding marriage and our roles in it, we can find the answer when we consult with His divine blueprint. God gave us the diagram for marriage by laying out His instructions in His Word. This is what He said:

"For this reason a man shall leave his father and his mother, and be joined to his wife; and they shall become one flesh." (Genesis 2:24)

This Scripture encapsulates God's view of marriage. When a man and woman are joined together they are no longer "me and you." They become "we." God considers the two individuals as one cohesive unit. As a result, sharing "one flesh" involves physical and spiritual intimacy and it is the greatest human bond that exists. It is even greater than the bond between a mother and child because without two parents first coming together, there can be no child.

But too often you and I abandon the divine blueprint and reject the design of God for our marriages. Both men and women are guilty of this. We set aside God's plan and adopt that which the world has offered us. Instead of listening to what God says about who we are as husbands and wives, we listen to the voices of society spouting secular wisdom. We would be so much better off if we understood that God has a purpose in mind and He wants that purpose to be fulfilled in us.

In case you're searching for the meaning of your relationship, find out by checking the divine blueprint. That way, whenever your marriage hits the wall of adversity, you and your mate will rise up with a stronger bond. I like to put it this way. As long as you're working with God's instructions, you'll bend where you're

When a Woman Loves a Man

supposed to bend and hold where you're supposed to hold.

If you want to be on the right side of life, you have to understand that God's view and the world's view are in direct opposition. The world says, "Until debt do us part," but God says, "Until death do us part."

Therefore, when God's Word of instruction is hidden in our hearts, we don't look for reasons to abandon the marriage, we unite in our determination to stay together. Marriages can endure until death because God designed them to. They don't because we have altered God's plan. We have made changes to the original blueprint and as usual we have created a mess. Financial problems may arise, but they don't make us want to get rid of each other. That's what the world says we ought to do. But the divine blueprint says, when a marriage faces trouble, a husband and wife can withstand it regardless of personality differences or disagreements. The marriage can endure to the end because that's the way God designed it.

To get a better picture of this, here is an illustration. The designer of an automobile will test his concept car to see if it will perform the way it was intended. He pays careful attention to every detail and meticulously crafts his design so that it meets his stringent specifications. In other words, he wants it to bend where it's supposed to bend and hold where it's supposed to hold. The ultimate goal is to put the finished product on display when it reflects the image he had in mind.

In a similar way, God made marriage the way He did so He could put it on display for the world to see. Did you know that godly marriage is a picture of Jesus Christ and His church? God has given us a priceless image of what a marriage is like when He's in control of it. When such a marriage is exhibited, people will know that Christ is in the midst of it. The two partners don't act like people without God in their lives. The relationship becomes a tested and proven representation of God's standard much the same way people can spot a Porsche when they see one. This was God's plan for marriage. People should look at a Christian marriage and see Christ.

As a woman who desires to be a virtuous woman, you want to know how to govern yourself. Don't consult with someone's philosophy or rely on anyone's educated opinion. If you want to know how to be a godly wife—don't talk to any woman or man. If you want to be a virtuous woman and godly wife, consult the Designer. There are godly women, mature women around, and the Bible tells them to instruct the younger women. But keep in mind that God is the ultimate and final answer. After all, it is His creation, and who knows it better than Him? When you're ready for the righteous answers, you must go back to the divine design and rely on the unadulterated Word of the living God to show you the way.

When you consult with the Divine Designer of the marriage institution, you will find that the wife was intricately fashioned in these three ways:

a) to fulfill the purpose God gave her
b) to prepare for her God-given role
c) to complete the life-giving process

Her Purpose

The overall design of God for a woman comes together in how she loves a man. Just as Adam was fulfilled in her, Eve was fulfilled in him. God's blueprint describes how He has created woman so that her role would reflect the reason for which He made her. She was equipped for the man that He was going to bring into her life.

Eve was given a specific role and certain things were expected of her. In fact, the first reference God made to Eve became her number one purpose. God said, "I will make him a helper suitable for him" (Genesis 2:18b).

So here we have it. Eve was designed to be her husband's helper. The reason her role was so special is because there are only two people called "helper" in the Bible. Eve was one of them, and you may be surprised to find that the other was God. Before He gave her to Adam, God instilled in the woman's design the ability to be a natural source of protection and support for her man. If you have ever wondered why women are natural nurturers and fiercely protective, now you know.

The word "helper" comes from the Hebrew word *ezer*, which

means "one who helps." It is used twenty-one times in the Old Testament. Now get this: nineteen times the word is used about God. The other two times it describes the woman. Please don't miss this. God has given woman a designation that she alone shares with Him.

Let me clear up any misunderstanding that may exist right here and now. The woman's role cannot have anything to do with inferiority because there's nothing inferior about God. She and God share a role and God is Supreme, Majestic, Magnificent, and Marvelous. God is everything that is good. He wouldn't give Himself a designation that would degrade Him.

Now think about how incredible this is. The woman alone shares the name that God has taken for Himself. To show you the tremendous effect this produces, I want to give you some examples of where that name is used in reference to God. Keep in mind some of the synonyms for the word "help" are "support," "rescue," "improve," "assist," and "relieve."

"Our soul waits for the Lord; He is our help [*ezer*] and our shield." (Psalm 33:20)

"God is our refuge and strength, a very present help [*ezer*] in trouble." (Psalm 46:1)

"But I am afflicted and needy; hasten to me, O God! You are my help [*ezer*] and my deliverer; O Lord, do not delay." (Psalm 70:5)

"I will lift up my eyes to the mountains; from where shall my help [*ezer*] come?" (Psalm 121:1)

Do you see the awesome power God has instilled in the workings of a virtuous woman? By calling both Him and the woman *ezer,* He has given the woman a position like none other. But I must point out the main distinction here. *Yahweh* is the Big Ezer and the woman that He created is the little ezer. You see, God wasn't going to supply some things for Adam. Through Eve, He could channel blessings to the man that was her counterpart.

As a result, there are some blessings that God has reserved for a husband that he will only get through his wife. God made Eve to protect Adam in certain ways and to cover his back. Because she was in relationship with God, guess what she was to remind Adam of when he looked at her? That's right, the Big Ezer.

Let me illustrate what I'm talking about. My oldest grandson, Little J, and I hang out together. We were on our way down to his daddy's barbershop so I could get a haircut. But first we stopped at the gas station. I had given him five dollars, and you know how it is when a five-year-old has five dollars in his pocket. He is rich and has a burning desire to start spending his wealth.

And so he said, "Papa?" I said, "What, man?" He said, "Papa, can I get a pop and some potato chips?" I said, "Yes, but you will wait." He got the *yes* part, but he had no interest in the *wait* part.

"Wait" doesn't register in the five-year-old brain.

As we were driving to his daddy's shop, he was blown up like a bull frog. I said, "What's the matter, man?" He said, "Nothing, Papa." Then he kind of rolled his eyes at me a little bit. I already knew what was wrong with him so I said, "You want a pop and potato chips and that five dollars is burning a hole in your pocket."

He said, "Yes, sir."

I said, "But I asked you to wait. Now let me tell you why I asked you to wait. We're going to your daddy's barber shop. And one of the things that your daddy has at his barber shop is pop and potato chips. Right? You were going to spend your own money to get what you want. But when we get to your daddy's shop, both of us are going to have free pop and chips."

He started smiling and said, "Oh yeah, so I keep my money and I still get pop and potato chips." I replied, "Now you've got it." His whole demeanor changed, because even a five-year-old understands free.

Let me explain. God is saying to us, "I'm the Big Ezer and I have insight and foresight that you don't have. You see, I have already calculated how we're going to get what you need so you can keep what I gave you. You don't have to worry about spending what I gave you because I'm going to get you what you want and it's not going to cost you anything."

For those of you who are single and desire a husband, know that you have God's virtue and God's virginity. You don't need to bargain. God is saying to you, "Look, I've got a blessing for you. You don't have to spend what I gave you because I'm going to give you what you want and I'm going to make sure it doesn't cost you anything."

It would be better for you to wait on God because it will be a blessing and not a constant headache. Notice I didn't say there would be *no* headache at all because that is not the reality. In life, there will be some headaches and we can't avoid that, but even with the headache, God supplies the headache reliever. But God doesn't want you to have to pay a large price for what He wants to freely give you.

Taking Care of Business

When you study the description of the virtuous woman, you will find out how the woman of virtue conducts herself. Here are some of the many activities that define this ideal individual. In verse 14, we find her willing to travel a distance to save money when she needs to make purchases that will benefit her family. She cuts coupons, shops at Aldi, and catches items on sale.

In verse 15, she gets up late at night and prepares dinner for her household. In verses 21 and 22, she is noted for her ability to make fine clothing for her family, and verse 27 says she lovingly watches over her home. She has learned skills that benefit her family, and she lovingly exercises those skills. As her husband and children observe the tender and adept care that she demonstrates, they are moved to praise her.

Some people may assert that this kind of woman doesn't even exist. Let's face it. There are women who don't embody the wives that God wants them to be. To make matters worse, their husbands aren't what God desires them to be either. Then life gets messy. The roles of the two mates are so intricately entwined that they need each other to function in a healthy and holistic manner.

But the point of Scripture providing all of these details is to set forth an example for godly women to emulate. The central idea of Proverbs 31 is that a wife is to be an asset to her husband and not a liability.

In stark contrast to such potential negativity, the Bible says that a good wife is trusted and revered by her husband. And contrary to what the skeptics may think, there are some very good examples of the virtuous wife.

You may have heard of the late Edward Victor Hill who is better known as Dr. E. V. Hill. Once at a pastors' conference I heard him say, "Well, I have had two wives." He explained that one was in heaven and one was on earth and that was far enough apart to keep him out of trouble. Then, referring to his deceased first wife, he said, "But I want to tell you about my baby." At that time he was combating with the gangs in Los Angeles. Someone sent

Dr. Hill an ominous note that read, "We're going to kill you. We're going to put a bomb in your car."

The next morning he awoke to the scrumptious aroma of the breakfast that was waiting for him. As he sat down to eat, he wondered, *Where's my baby?* When she finally entered the room, he told her that he was getting ready to go out. He said, "Don't worry, if I blow up, you'll be well taken care of." Then she handed him his keys and told him the car wasn't going to blow up. She informed him, "I went out this morning and started the car to make sure that there was no bomb about to go off." Amazingly, she was willing to put her own life on the line to save his.

Here is another good illustration. It is said that Winston Churchill's marriage was considered one of the best examples of trust and loyalty in England. Before he would give a speech in the House of Commons, he wouldn't even begin until he got a sign from her. The story goes that later on in life he was asked the question in an interview, "Mr. Churchill, if you could live again, what would you want to be?" With a twinkle in his eye, Churchill simply replied, "Mrs. Churchill's next husband." What a testimony!

These women exemplified what Proverbs 31:12 has to say about a woman who loves her man: "She does him good and not evil all the days of her life."

Attitude Matters

Not only will an excellent wife treat her husband well by her deeds and actions, he will reap the benefit of her righteous attitude. Her approach will be that she only wants the best for her husband. Can you see how a woman of virtue functions as a channel through which God sends blessings?

Notice also that the Scripture says the virtuous woman will regard her husband in this way all of her life, not his life. In other words, after he is dead and gone, the memory of that man will still dwell within her. She will honor him even when she's not in his presence.

Her Preparation

The reason a woman can display such a confident and supportive demeanor is because of the innate ability she possesses. Here we get a glimpse of the circumstances surrounding God's preparation for her. It tells me that, even before Adam was aware of his incomplete state, God anticipated his need and planned for it. Here is how the Word of God describes the situation before Eve came into being.

"Out of the ground the Lord God formed every beast of the field and every bird of the sky, and brought them to the man to see what he would call them; and whatever the man called a living creature, that was its name.

The man gave names to all the cattle, and to the birds of the sky, and to every beast of the field, but for Adam there was not found a helper suitable for him." (Genesis 2:19–20)

We see that Adam's wife was in the mind of God before she was ever in the arms of Adam. Moreover, Adam was numb to his need until God had him name the animals in nature. As he went through the garden doing what God had commanded him, it became apparent that none of the creatures could match Adam's intellect, character, ethical abilities, and spirituality. Adam was faithful in his service to God, and it was time for him to be rewarded.

I cannot help but wonder, *Was he looking for a woman? What did he know about a spouse?* I suppose we will never know. But one thing the Bible does tell us—there was not one found for him. Without a doubt, God created that desire in Adam. Here is the principle. He was committed to God first and, as a result of his dedication, God added to him a companion for life.

FOR SINGLES ONLY

This is a note specifically for the women who are single. Please know that you've got to be very careful and wait for the one God has prepared for you. Otherwise, if you're too inpatient and impulsive to wait, you will wind up taking the first thing coming with two legs and a pair of pants. Let me caution you. If you do that, you'd better check first to see if there's a wallet in his pocket. And that it's not empty.

I've said this to single women before, and it's important enough to repeat. You need to get off of the yellow brick road of relationships, messing with scarecrows, folks that have no brains. Stop playing around with tin men who don't have a heart. Stop wasting your time with cowardly lions; by that I mean, men who will slap you. Otherwise, you'll wind up looking for love in all the wrong places.

Prayerfully, you will be able to avoid the inherent trauma of being in such dire circumstances. As a single person, your primary focus should be on your ministry to God. It is out of the context of your service to Him that God is going to do for you whatever you need Him to do. But the reality is, many of you are seeking a spouse instead of seeking to serve and that's what will prevent you from finding the right mate. You have never been instructed to search for a spouse. The Bible tells us that if we delight ourselves in the Lord, He will give us the desires of our heart. Our hearts will desire what delights God. You will want what God wants and what He wants for you. If you're not careful you could get an Ishmael instead of an Isaac because God is only going to give His best when you put Him first.

Furthermore, be cautious of folks who tell single people that they shouldn't want anybody but God. The implication is that

When a Woman Loves a Man

God wants them to be single. (Have you noticed that this usually comes from married people?) Guess what? Adam had God—and God provided a companion for him. After all, God is the One who said it wasn't good for man to be alone. Following God's order is what's really important. Scripture says to

> "Seek first His kingdom and His righteousness, and all these things will be added to you." (Matthew 6:33)

It doesn't say to seek only God; just seek Him first and He will fulfill the desires of your heart.

This is what preparation is all about. When you're standing in a position of righteousness, then He'll line you up with the right mate for you. So, don't worry, it's all right to want to be married; it's not all right to pick your own spouse. Trust me, you'll mess it up. Just do it God's way and you'll get the right results.

Her Process

Everything that God does is for a reason and all things are done in the proper season. Have you ever noticed that He takes us through a process before we receive a blessing? That's God's way. The process He went through to create the woman followed this same pattern. Here's what happened.

"So the Lord God caused a deep sleep to fall upon the man, and he slept; then He took one of his ribs and closed up the flesh at that place. The Lord God fashioned into a woman the rib which He had taken from the man, and brought her to the man." (Genesis 2:21–22)

Notice the method God used in the process of making the woman. He put Adam to sleep. My good friend Kenny Grant once said and I will repeat it: "Man will never fully understand woman because we were asleep when God made her." I believe that's about as good an explanation that we'll ever have in describing the differences between the two sexes.

But God knew that we would need each other. Scripture says here that God produced the woman from the man by taking one of Adam's ribs and fashioning Eve. The Bible actually says that God *yatsa* the woman for the man. The Hebrew word *yatsa* can be translated into the word "built." So God literally built the woman for the man, according to His divine design. Then He presented her to Adam.

Remember, everything else that God created came from the dirt, including Adam. But the woman did not. This time God used a piece of the man's flesh and bone.

Now, here is a divine rule of which women must be aware. Every man who has a wife or will have one in the future must be willing to give something up because Adam had to give something up. He gave up a rib, according to the Bible, and with that action God

When a Woman Loves a Man

established this fundamental principle that actually applies to both men and women: Give to God what you have as a sacrifice and allow God to give you what you need in return.

For example, recall the account of the fish and the loaves in John 6:5–13. Jesus took the boy's fish and loaves, multiplied them, and fed the multitude. Although it wasn't enough, it was all that the boy had to offer. Through this object lesson, Jesus demonstrated that God is not concerned about what you don't have; rather, He's concerned about whether you are willing to offer whatever you do have. In His own way and timing, He will increase it and give you back more than you could even imagine.

You may be feeling overwhelmed and at the end of your rope, you may be feeling as though you can't go on. Give God those feelings; He can handle them for you. If you need to give Him your pride or your will, do that and the God of all grace will strengthen your relationship and increase your marriage in wonderful ways. Or, if you are a single woman, offer Him your heart and He will grant you the desires of your heart.

As I study Scripture, whether the thing you have to give is something good or bad—it works both ways. God will take what you put on the altar and give you back whatever you need. You can rest assured that it will be more than what you sacrificed for Him.

Think *about it:*

1. Are you satisfied with the personal relationship that you share with the Lord?
2. In what ways can you make improvements that will bring you closer to God?
3. Based on the Proverbs 31 description, tell in your own words what it means to be a virtuous woman.
4. How well do you understand your husband's needs? Do you think that you were adequately prepared to be the wife that your husband needs?
5. In what areas do you think you could better satisfy the expectations your husband has for you as his wife?
6. Have you prayed consistently for God to give you a strategy that will change you in these areas?

Live *by it:*

Dear Heavenly Father, give your precious ones Your bountiful grace as they show a desire to follow Your divine blueprint. As the most gracious Helper that You are, You embody the divine design that You desire all women to emulate. Teach them how to become the helper and support their husbands need so that You can channel blessings to their mates and bless their marriages, in Christ's name. So be it.

When a Woman Loves a Man

when a woman loves *a man,*

she completes and complements him

the total package

HAVE YOU HEARD the story about the man who died and his wife wanted him to speak to her from the grave? She went to a medium and said,

"Would you call up my husband, Bill?"

So the medium called up the spirit of Bill, and his wife was able to talk to him.

The wife said, "Bill, Bill is that you?"

He answered, "Yes, it's me."

Then she asked, "Bill, are you happy where you are?"

"Yes, I am," he replied.

She continued to question him. "Bill, are you happier where you are now than when you were with me?"

He said, "Infinitely so."

She asked, "Well, Bill, tell me what heaven is like?"

He responded, "Who's in heaven?"

Sounds like this man was so glad to be relieved of his wife that he didn't care in which direction he would spend eternity. Sadly, this is a reflection of how some marriages end up. But, typically that's not how it all begins. On the day a couple marries, she is radiantly beautiful and looks like a queen. Then, after five years or so, something unfortunate happens.

Proverbs 12:4 could possibly shed some light on the situation. For it states, "An excellent wife is the crown of her husband, but she who shames him is like rottenness in his bones."

From this Scripture we understand the difference between the two opposite approaches that a woman can take toward her marriage. By her attitude and actions, she can either be a crown or a cancer. She can either be a healer or a hell-raiser; a complimenter or a complainer. In addition, she can be a nurturer or a nagger; a helper or a hinderer to her husband. The distinction is found in whether a wife understands who she is in the sight of God and her spouse.

According to Proverbs 12:4, a virtuous woman is a crown on

When a Woman Loves a Man

her husband's head. If I take a crown and put it on a man's head, what does that make him? A king. And if he is a king, what does that make his wife? That's right, a queen.

If you decide to be a crown, then you will reflect the qualities of a crown. A crown is a symbol of royalty; it is regal. It symbolizes a prize to the one who is privileged to wear it. It represents the highest pinnacle of success, dignity, and excellence.

To be consistent with this description, a wife would behave in ways that encourage and elevate her husband. Crowned with dignity and self-respect, she would convey that same level of distinction to her mate by building him up in every way possible. As a result, she would be a superior companion. That is how God intends for those of us in marriage relationships to live out His Word.

THE QUESTION OF IDENTITY— WHO ARE YOU?

Can you imagine the trouble people can get into when they don't know who they are and whose they are? Spiritually speaking, this is the fundamental reason why marriages end in failure.

The first thing any of us needs to understand is that we belong to the Lord Jesus. In the case of a married woman, her second commitment must be to her husband—if she is to function in the role that the Lord has given her. Therefore, if you are a wife who desires to fulfill the purpose that was intricately designed for you, you first have to embrace your identity and conduct yourself in view of the role God has given you.

Recall the passage in Genesis 2:18–24 that depicts the account of God when He determined to create the woman. Let me give you a brief recap: After He caused a deep sleep to come over Adam, God took one of the man's ribs, closed up his flesh, and put the brother back together. Then God used that part of the man and formed the woman. But something very intricate and deeply probing occurred through this creative process. You may be surprised to find that the woman's identity becomes lost in who God made the man to be.

If you don't believe me, then let the Bible speak for itself. Scripture says that God brought her to the man and Adam called her "woman" (Genesis 2:23). But in Genesis 5:2, God called the two of them by one name: "He created them male and female, and He blessed them and named them Man in the day when they were created." Notice the word "Man" is singular. God gave them one name and the name that He chose belonged to Adam. Clearly, when a man and woman join together in wedlock, it is God's intention for the two people to share the man's identity. That's why the woman takes the man's last name.

The Word of God expresses what has taken place in this way,

"For this reason a man shall leave his father and his mother, and be joined to his wife; and they shall become one flesh." (Genesis 2:24)

When a Woman Loves a Man

Consequently, when God knitted the woman's identity to the man, He sealed her commitment to her husband.

In spiritual terms, what does that mean in regard to the wife? There are five aspects of what transpires when a woman makes her marriage vows. They are:

1. *Her old identity as a single woman is dead, and she is reborn with the man's identity.* Isn't that what we say about the new birth? When we are in Christ, our former identity no longer exists (2 Corinthians 5:17). Through the baptizing work of the Holy Spirit, we are dead to our old nature, buried with Christ, and raised in the newness of life. This is the process that takes us out of the old, sinful Adam and places us in the new resurrected Adam; that is, Christ Jesus.

Jesus took the picture of our relationship with Him, duplicated it, and gave that picture to the wedded couple as a special gift. This symbolism is captured when a wife takes her husband's last name. Through their marriage union, the woman is now dead to her old life and old name. She has been raised in the newness of a married life with her husband.

For instance, if I were to present my wife and myself to you on some occasion, I would say we are Mr. and Mrs. James Ford Jr. It would be inappropriate to introduce the two of us as Mr. and Mrs. James and Leslie Ford. According to God's law concerning the union of marriage, when my wife assumed my name, her previous identity became lost in who I am.

2. Whether a woman realizes it or not, taking the name of her husband is a pledge of allegiance to him. By this gesture, she is now declaring that her father no longer comes first in her life. She is signaling to her husband that, from now on, he is the number one man in her life.

I want to caution those of you who are having trouble with this idea because you haven't made daddy number two yet. It's a violation of God's plan if you're still putting your father before your mate. This is a sure sign of not fully connecting with your God-given role as a wife.

Now, here's a newsflash for you. In order for a marriage to work as God intended, a man must cut the apron strings of his mama and a woman must cut the purse strings of her daddy. And please don't say, "I can't get another daddy, but I can always get another husband." Well, not if you honor God's Word because God never approved of divorce; He only allowed it.

This was our Lord's explanation when Jesus was questioned about divorce in Matthew 19:8: "Because of your hardness of heart Moses permitted you to divorce your wives; but from the beginning it has not been this way." Clearly, it was not God's intention for people to sever their marriages. Making your husband your number one priority is God's way. Wives who think it's all right to compromise their vows just might end up back at home with daddy.

3. Authority and submission go hand in hand. Assuming the

husband's identity is the first act of a woman's submission. In biblical times, whenever someone was given a name, the person who did the naming held the authority.

For example, God gave Adam the authority to designate the names of the animals; it was an outward sign that Adam had dominion over God's creation. When Eve arrived, God also allowed Adam to name her. This too was a sign of the man's authority over the woman. Subsequently, when a wife accepts her husband's name, it is a symbol of her submission to him.

4. *A change in the woman's identity highlights the perpetual nature of submission.* It becomes a matter of duration. How long should my wife submit to me? As long as her last name is Ford. The length of time is verbally proclaimed as the couple making their marriage vows declares, "Until death do us part."

5. *A change in identity is the symbol of a total commitment to the spiritual principles of marriage.* When a wife takes the husband's last name at the altar, it signifies the first fruits of her pledge to him. In other words, it is the commencement of the spiritual principles that the couple will follow in their marriage union.

Unfortunately, here's what we see too often. Christians have allowed the world to pull us into its secular concept of marriage and, as a result, God's Word has been denigrated. The order that God established from the beginning has been compromised. We live in a day now where women have "come a long way, baby." Now the woman's role has evolved to the point that she has to make the bacon, fry it up, and too often she has to eat it all by herself.

This is not the total package God had in mind. And it's a sad thing when the principles of Scripture are violated because someone has to pay the price. God didn't give these principles for His benefit. He gave them for our benefit. He made the two genders the way He did for a reason. But the reality is that there's a lot of pressure on women today because they're doing things God never called them to do.

We Christians need to do our homework and take the time to understand God's standards. If we want to be successful, we must be careful to follow the natural order that He predetermined. I always say that God gave the man broad shoulders to bear burdens and the woman broad hips to bear babies. We're different because God designed us that way. And the way He designed things to work is still the best way.

For instance, Leslie and I travel to Portland because I serve as an adjunct professor at a Bible college in Cannon Beach. We stay at a beautiful place located right on the Pacific Ocean. There is a huge glass door in the accommodation that looks out on a magnificent fireplace. After I teach my last class in the evening, we look forward to enjoying the beautiful spectacle that it offers. We get ourselves some popcorn and sparkling grape juice. Then we sit up and talk for hours as we watch that awesome view.

Now the fire, with its glowing wonder, is exquisite. Fire can be very romantic when it is contained and fulfilling the function for which God designed it. But on the other hand, if the fire were to ignite the curtains, that would turn into a tragedy. Right? Fire is only a good thing when it's contained within the parameters that God established its goodness.

It's the same with the divine principles for marriage. They're here for a reason. God wants you to have beauty and romance in your life so you can express yourself to the optimum. But when you step outside of the parameters and go against His principles, just like with an out-of-control fire, you'll have to call 911. If you allow yourself to get into a heated marital debate, you will need some help from heaven to put out those fiery tongues and actions. Why? There is a marriage commitment at risk of being burned beyond repair.

When a woman loves a man, she will live out God's principles and do whatever is necessary to conduct her marriage according to God's plan.

What's Your Name?

Let me give you an example to show how some women struggle with the idea of giving up their premarital identity. I once received a letter from one of the ladies in my congregation, and this is what she shared with me. She heard my teaching on the concept of submission, with the first act being to take the husband's name in marriage. As a result, this sister really got convicted. She confessed that for thirty years of her marriage she had carried a hyphenated last name.

I was glad to hear that God had ministered to her and she was ready to drop her maiden name. Finally, this woman told me something that many women have to come to grips with. She admitted that when she first got married, she wouldn't have even listened to my message because it wouldn't have made sense to her.

Allow me to ask all the married ladies who have chosen to identify themselves by their maiden name: When are you going to stop living as if you don't belong to the man that you belong to? When are you going to start believing that God has given you a very precise role in your marriage? Marriage was designed by God; as a result, He set the standard. There are no two ways about it—embracing His mind-set is integral to accepting an overall commitment to your marriage.

You're the Woman for the Job

In my many years of marriage counseling, I've heard some shocking stories that have left me wondering about this question: Why do some women marry? My musing has caused me to study God's Word in depth about the subject of marriage and I've reached this conclusion. Before a woman can truly love her husband, she has to know how to fulfill her role as his wife. So many people enter marriage blindly and without a clue as to what they're getting into. They don't understand that it is impossible for a woman to make effective decisions about her relationship without regard for God's design of a wife.

I'm referring to certain specifications that are inherent in the marriage contract. When God made you a helpmate for your husband, He intended for you to meet two needs for your husband: to complete and complement him. And as long as you approach your responsibilities in this way, you are doing your part in making the marriage follow the pattern that God established.

For those of you who are career-oriented, let me put the rest of this discussion in the form of a résumé.

OBJECTIVE:
To Complete and Complement My Husband

MANY ARE THE ROLES OF A WIFE

I am convinced of this: when a woman loves a man in the way that God wants her to, she can make a bad man a good man. Moreover, she can make a good man a great man, simply by taking every opportunity to build the man up.

God will help her be the "helper" He designed a wife to be. By focusing on the specific functions that allow her to complete and complement her husband, she will be:

  a) a supplement to her husband
  b) a support for her husband
  c) strength for her husband
  d) security for her husband
  e) a sustainer for her husband

The first thing you have to remember is that God wants to bring blessings to your husband that will only come through you. Moreover, they will be fruitful blessings which will benefit you and your marriage. But He can only do it when you are in agreement with His plan. So when you get the wife component on track and he gets the husband part going in the right direction, together the two of you make up the total marriage package that God had in mind. And it's a beautiful thing.

Completer-in-Chief

As his wife, your first duty is to complete your husband. If you're wondering what this actually means, God intends for you to act as a supplement to him. For example, perhaps you are one of the many people who take a daily multivitamin supplement because it is a way of adding to your body whatever nutrients and minerals that

When a Woman Loves a Man

may be missing or doesn't have enough of. Some doctors recommend this practice as part of a regimen of staying healthy and whole. If a body is lacking in iron, it will draw strength from the iron supplied by the vitamin. The body's needs are fulfilled with the help of the vitamin supplement.

You see, God is saying this: "You need to stop complaining about what's missing in him. It's probably what you are supposed to be supplying. He needs your support. He needs your strength to sustain him and back him up. He needs you to supplement him and make him feel secure as only a wife can. These are the things that constitute your role as a helper to your husband. The reason that I gave him to you is because he needs to be whole and you can provide everything that he's missing."

Man has an instinctive desire for that which only a woman can provide. Let me explain how it all came about. God left an intrinsic need in Adam when He took a part from him to create Eve. When God gave Eve to be Adam's partner, he regained the missing part of himself back. He was complete again, but he also got something else.

Eve's existence became a supplement, an addition for Adam. What she brought to him was extra special. He got what he needed because Eve was made from what he had lost. She wasn't baggage; she was beauty. Eve was not intended to bring pain; she was a blessing—a gift from God.

Through marriage, God has provided for the completion of the husband through his wife—his helper—his little ezer. You see, whatever is found missing in the man, she will have it because she was made out of it.

Therefore, if he's quiet, she will be loud. If he's loud, she will be quiet. If he's an introvert, she will be an extrovert. If he's an extrovert, she will be an introvert. If he's quick tempered, she will have a slow fuse. If he's got a slow fuse, she will have a quick temper. If he has poor financial skills, she will have a degree in finance. This is math at its best: God's mathematical formula makes *two* become *one*.

Somebody ought to show their appreciation and tell God, "Thank You." He wants you to understand the blessing that is your marriage union. In his role, your husband is unique before God. He is also a channel of blessings and, without him, nothing happens in the marriage. It cannot function properly as a whole. I know that this may sound obvious, but a wife cannot have children without him—if you know what I mean. Hello, somebody.

Home Sweet Home

I think we are already aware of some very distinct ways in which God has defined the roles of the two genders. When God created the woman to be a blessing to the man, He gave her an instinctive need to supply what makes the relationship a complete entity. As a result, a virtuous wife will intuitively emphasize the ways that her femininity accentuates her husband's masculinity.

In a practical sense, it is embedded in her job description to be a nurturer. Nurturing takes place on all levels of life, especially life at home. Doesn't everything that pertains to your everyday living begin at home? Think about it. Home life is the nucleus around which all other activities revolve. It's the place where you eat, sleep, relax, entertain, and tend to your personal needs.

Although I'm not just speaking of doing household chores and cooking meals, it is clear that God assigned the responsibility of keeping the home to the wife. From a managerial point of view, a wife is to ensure the house runs in a decent and orderly manner. He has equipped women with an inborn ability to create a nurturing, comfortable environment in which the entire family can feel cared for and content. In the book of Titus, we find some important instructions about God's expectations of a wife who supports her husband by tending to her household:

> "Older women likewise are to be reverent in their behavior, not malicious gossips nor enslaved to much wine, teaching what is good, so that they may encourage the young women to love their husbands, to love their children, to be sensible, pure, workers at home, kind, being subject to their own husbands, so that the word of God will not be dishonored."
> (Titus 2:3–5)

The apostle Paul instructed Titus to see that God's order for Christian living was kept intact. When the wives were addressed, it was the older women who were given the responsibility to make sure that the younger women knew how to conduct themselves within the framework of their families. Besides the admonishment to keep their homes running smoothly, Paul's instructions included everything from how to treat their children, using good judgment, having pure motives, and submitting to their husbands.

Most importantly, his reason why women should follow these orders was, "so that the Word of God would not be dishonored." This is what needs to be emphasized. We spend too much time debating whether or not women should work outside of the home, who should handle the finances, whether Christian children should be homeschooled or sent to public school. The issue is women understanding and fulfilling their God-given roles in the marriage. When that happens, all of these other things are not that big to decide, because decisions will be made based on what's best for the family. It's not necessarily the issues that cause problems, but usually the way the decisions are being made. In other words, Paul made it clear that this was not his mandate; rather, it's about revering God. Now, who could argue with that?

On the flip side, when these qualities are not evident in a wife, she will not only bring reproach upon her husband—she will bring reproach upon our Lord by disobeying the Word of God.

Who would want to be found guilty of that?

People are always watching Christians to see if they practice what they preach. You may have heard someone say, "She calls herself a Christian . . ." One way that a wife can be found guilty of being labeled this way is when somebody observes her ungodly behavior toward her husband. Or, you might hear that phrase if her house is less than tidy.

Or, how about this one: "She calls herself a Christian, and she's got one of the worst attitudes you ever want to see in a woman." Hopefully, you can say "Amen" and not "Ouch" to these accusations.

And so it is her very presence in his life that makes a woman the supplement that her husband needs. Keep in mind that if you are not supplementing your husband you are harming him and your household. Because of the way in which men and women were designed, it's what makes him a whole being. Here is what Proverbs 19:14 says about it:

> "House and wealth are an inheritance from fathers, but a prudent wife is from the Lord."

King Solomon penned these words. As a man who had a thousand women, I suspect he knew a little bit about the fairer species. Some of the synonyms for the word "prudent" are "sensible," "practical," and "wise." Solomon's point is that God, in His immeasurable wisdom, can be trusted to provide a wife who possesses these virtuous attributes. It stands to reason that the man who acknowledges the Heavenly Father when he's looking for a wife won't be disappointed.

Some people have said that a good woman is hard to find, but listen to what King Solomon also had to say in Proverbs 18:22: "He who finds a wife finds a good thing and obtains favor from the Lord."

So ladies, God has given you the role of completer so that you and your husband can have a successful marriage that basks in the favor of God. If you trust Him as your Lord and Savior, He won't disappoint you. This is the way God designed marriage so that both of you will reap the benefits of the favor God gives your husband.

However, sustaining a warm and inviting home can be a challenge, and there are definitely times when a prudent wife is called on to supplement her husband's weaknesses. So at this moment, you may think that it's an impossible task to love your husband the way God wants you to. And you are correct if you're going to take on the responsibility all by yourself.

But remember, God knows better than you do. The only way to successfully show love to someone when it seems to be an insurmountable test is to rely on God's grace. It's like the angel told Mary—keep this Word close to your heart— *"for nothing will be*

When a Woman Loves a Man

impossible with God" (Luke 1:37). Always remember, God is your Helper just as He made you your mate's helper.

"Complementer"-in-Chief

Please forgive me; I just made up a word. But it describes what it takes to make up the total marriage package. The other critical component to the wife's role is to complement her husband. The word is defined as "to fill up, complete, or make perfect." Doesn't this sound like the role that the Holy Spirit plays in our lives? Well, it just so happens that, as a wife, you are to imitate the Holy Spirit when it comes to your husband.

Think of what the Holy Spirit does for us. He is the Comforter, which means that He encourages those who need to be uplifted. Furthermore, the Holy Spirit has the ability to sustain us when we're feeling weak. He comes alongside the downtrodden and supplies the hope they need. He shields us from things that could potentially harm us.

That is also what a wife must do for her husband—provide a sense of security and support. After being out there in the world working every day, he needs a lot of encouragement and protection from outside forces. I tell you, in society, men have been castrated. A man has to be twice as good to go half as far, getting beat on, bruised, and battered all along the way.

Men don't need to come home and get that same kind of

treatment. His home should be his castle, a shelter from the storm. Everyone should welcome the king back to his castle. Because so much of a man's identity is tied to his vocation, it is important for the woman who loves him to affirm him in it and assure him that his contribution is valuable and wanted. A woman who minimizes his contributions to the family maximizes his vulnerability to being appreciated somewhere else.

Although he may not be the perfect mate, when he comes home from working like a Hebrew slave and the world has flooded in on him, this is the time for his wife to come alongside him and say, "Hi, baby, how was your day? Come on in and let me make this home your palace because you're the king. You're home now and I'm ready to take care of you, baby."

Being a complement to your husband is God's desire for a married woman, and He wants you to provide relief for your man. See, wife, when you function in your role as God would have it, marriage is called wedlock, not deadlock. It's supposed to be about matrimony not acrimony. Because the word "acrimony" means to be harsh and bitter in your attitude, your actions, and your speech that is exactly the opposite of the kind of communication God expects.

Part of your role is to encourage him to fulfill his purpose; he was made to be the breadwinner. But, Lord knows, that can be a difficult way to go. God wants you to use the creativity He gave you to find ways that celebrate your man. He wants you to give him the courage and confidence that he needs. Fill him up with compliments, and help him to be a better husband—even if you have to do it by faith for a while. You married him for a reason. There were some things about him that made you want to marry him and you need to remember that. If nothing else, remember God designed the both of you and He knew exactly what He was doing.

I say this all the time: Beside every good man there is a tired wife and a surprised mother-in-law. When you understand that you are his support system, you can make your good man become the great man God designed him to be. A woman who loves her man can relate to the sentiment of the world renowned country music artist Tammy Wynette, who encouraged women to "stand by your man."

Let me give you an example. My greatest support comes from my wife. One evening when she and I were at a restaurant having dinner, we encountered two very distinguished men of God. These gentlemen are veterans of the Word of God who have been in the trenches of spiritual warfare longer than some of us have lived.

One of them, Dr. Melvin Banks, said, "There's Pastor Ford. He spoke at Urban Ministries and, boy, he lit the place up. We had to turn on the sprinkler system because we didn't want all our paper material to burn up." I just laughed. Then he said to my wife, "You know, he's a great preacher, probably one of the greatest I've ever heard." My wife replied, "I know."

I thought to myself, *Oh no, she didn't say that.* But she wasn't finished yet. She continued, "That's right, he studies and the Lord blesses him. He's my favorite teacher too." Later on when we were alone, I said to her, "Baby, you were just supposed to say thank you." She said, "Well, I just told the truth, that's all."

AVOID THE PITFALLS

Let me be the first one to tell you that marriage can be hard work; particularly, if you're trying to do it God's way. It's no secret that you'll face opposition. The enemy doesn't want you to succeed. So take caution and don't give him any ammunition that he can use against you.

For example, look at the story of David and Michal in the books of 1 and 2 Samuel. It portrays an example of what can occur when a wife is remiss in her duties to complete and complement her mate. Her lack of loyalty becomes painfully apparent and detrimental to her life and the marriage she was given to protect.

When their story began, Saul was king of Israel. He had promised that the man who killed the giant, Goliath, could marry his daughter (1 Samuel 17:25). We all know David was that man. Although she had fallen in love with David, Saul only agreed to allow Michal to marry David because he was jealous of him and hoped that David would soon be killed. Saul set him up in a battle with the Philistines, but David prevailed and killed two hundred men just to win Michal (1 Samuel 18:27). And so they were married.

After that, David and Saul became archenemies. Scripture gives this account of David's wife when she had his back.

> "Then Saul sent messengers to David's house to watch him, in order to put him to death in the morning. But Michal, David's wife, told him, saying, 'If you do not save your life tonight, tomorrow you will be put to death.'" (1 Samuel 19:11)

Notice in this verse that Michal is called the wife of David. She was looking out for her husband as any wife should. Her husband's safety was her first priority, and she helped him to escape Saul's wrath—even at the cost of jeopardizing her relationship with her father. She was putting her husband first.

At this point in their lives, Michal was acting as her husband's helper. She was cooperating with the Holy Spirit, who was protecting David from Saul's attempts to kill him.

But time brings on a change and so much drama transpired in their lives. Saul's pursuit continued and David was constantly on the run. Eventually, the two split up and Michal married someone else. Then after Saul was killed, David became king and commanded her to come back to him.

However, at that time, Michal was no longer the devoted wife of their youth. In fact, she despised David. Check out these next verses that describe her state of mind.

> "Then it happened as the ark of the Lord came into the city of David that Michal the daughter of Saul looked out of the window and saw King David leaping and dancing before the Lord; and she despised him in her heart. But when David returned to bless his household, Michal the daughter of Saul came out to meet David and said, 'How the king of Israel distinguished himself today! He uncovered himself today in the eyes of his servants' maids as one of the foolish ones shamelessly uncovers himself!' So David said to Michal, 'It was before the Lord, who chose me above your father and above all his house, to appoint me ruler over the people of the Lord, over Israel; therefore I will celebrate before the Lord. 'I will be more lightly esteemed than this and will be humble in my own eyes, but with the maids of whom you have spoken, with them I will be distinguished.' Michal the daughter of Saul had no child to the day of her death." (2 Samuel 6:16, 20–23)

Now what is wrong in this passage? Did you notice that three times this woman was referred to as Michal, the daughter of Saul? There's a predicament here. God's Word indicates that He's got a problem with something. No longer is she referred to as David's wife. This story pinpoints two contrasting attitudes a wife holds

When a Woman Loves a Man

toward her husband. Why does the Word of God call her David's wife in the beginning of their relationship? Then after she came against her husband, she was called Michal, the daughter of Saul.

Here's what was going on. Number one, in the beginning, she was more committed to her husband than she was to her father, which is the way that a woman should be. When her father wanted to kill her husband, she realized that her obligation was first to her husband and not to her daddy. So she went against her father to protect her husband. This is what a wife is supposed to do. She was David's wife. As his support system, she was looking out for his best interest. She did him good and not evil.

Number two. There was a great deal of history between the two of them. But the final straw seemed to come about when Michal became dissatisfied with David because he was worshipping God too much. She watched in disdain as David danced and praised God and felt that he was making a fool of himself. And so three times the Bible says she was no longer acting like the wife of David. She was acting like the daughter of Saul, showing her loyalty to her father and not to her husband. Michal developed a bitter hatred toward David that was also reflected in her relationship with God.

Let me add that her life did not have to become such a disappointment. In His infinite mercy, God would have turned her situation around had she turned to Him. But instead, the Bible says that Michal, the daughter of Saul, had no child. What does that tell you?

Children are a heritage, the fruit of a womb. So God's response to the disrespect of her husband was to deny her what every Jewish woman wanted to do—produce a male child. Tragically, God closed her womb because she wasn't rightly related to David. She did not complete the image of a wife that God intended her to fulfill.

My prayer is for every wife who needs to ask her husband's forgiveness for a lack of commitment to him. If everybody else can get you to do something but him, there's a problem. The boss at the job just needs to tell you what to do and you do it. If Daddy calls you, you're gone. Yet If all your husband wants is for you to make him a sandwich, are you guilty of saying something like, "Fix your own sandwich. You've got two hands."

Please hear what the Lord is saying to you right now and take heed. Look at yourself in the mirror and then look at the picture of a wife that God has given in His Word. Do they match up? When a woman loves a man, she completes him. She complements him in a way that together they make up God's design for the total marriage package.

Think *about it*:

1. Before reading this chapter, did you realize that a wife takes on the identity of her husband when they marry?
2. Have you ever struggled with giving up your premarital identity?

When a Woman Loves a Man

3. What are some of the differences between the secular concept of marriage and God's view of marriage?
4. Do you embrace the biblical view that it is the woman's responsibility to keep the home?
5. In what ways do you satisfy your husband's need for support? From this chapter, did you learn any new information on how to provide a sense of security for him?

Live *by it*:

Dear Heavenly Father, I thank You for the gift of marriage. I ask now that You bless every woman who is reading these words. I pray that those who are wives will receive Your Word on how to fulfill the role You have given them. Help them to understand how to be the queen, the crown of glory upon their husbands' heads, in Christ's name. So be it.

when a woman loves *a man,*
she submits to his headship

perfect submission

THE STORY IS TOLD about a guy who was speeding down the highway. An officer chased him a couple of miles and finally caught up with him.

At first the officer said, "Man, what is your problem?" Then he thought about it and recanted, "No. I don't even want to hear it. I've heard it all. As a matter of fact, if you can tell me something that I haven't already heard, then I'll just issue you a warning ticket."

The man responded, "Well, my wife ran off with a police officer. When I noticed you were chasing me, I thought you were trying to catch me so you could give her back to me."

So he got a warning ticket.

That is a humorous little anecdote and sometimes a little humor is good for the soul. But, on the other hand, marriage is serious business, and God is not playing games. If it were possible to peer inside the relationship that this man and wife shared, no doubt the marriage wasn't lining up with God's blueprint. When marriages are in agreement with His prescribed plan, husbands and wives don't want to run away from each other and abandon their marriages. Rather, they share the strongest human bond on earth and that makes them stay together in love—through thick and thin.

Both partners have a role in making the marriage work. So, of course, it would be misguiding to offer a complete discussion about a virtuous woman and how she loves her man without including the subject of submission. I know this is a detested word among women, but it is fundamental to the relationship between a wife and her husband. Because when a woman loves a man, she understands that it is part of her role to submit to his headship.

A MIRROR IMAGE

Before I move on, let me briefly explain the concept of submission here. I cover it in detail in my book *Seven Reasons Why God Created Marriage*, which discusses the functional order that Paul defines in 1 Corinthians 11:3. This is what he wrote: "I want you to understand that Christ is the head of every man, and the man is the head of a woman, and God is the head of Christ." Here Scripture brings the Trinity into view and helps us to recognize that the essence of equality exists in a marital relationship along with a distinction of function. In other words, two married people are equal in every way although they have very different roles to play.

In this way, the relationship between a husband and wife resembles the equality of the Trinity. The three members of the Godhead are equal yet they all function in a unique way. The reason why this is important for a married couple to understand is because the members of the Trinity illuminate the idea of voluntary submission to one another. That's why Paul drew the comparison between God's Trinity and a marital union.

IT'S ALL GOOD

Now, what was the result of God's actions when He made the woman to correspond with the man? We have established that God's intended purpose was that the husband would be the wife's authority. Consequently, wives are admonished to be submissive to their husbands. First Peter 3:1 makes this very clear.

"In the same way, you wives, be submissive to your own husbands so that even if any of them are disobedient to the word, they may be won without a word by the behavior of their wives."

The apostle Peter issued a very specific instruction here and he didn't mince his words: A wife's primary focus is to submit to her husband. Furthermore, he stressed that a woman is to carry out her responsibility of submission regardless of whether the man obeys God's Word or not.

Now I know that in today's world the word "submit" is a dirty six-letter word. But in fact, the Hebrew word for "submit" comes from a military term that means to "order under." Therefore, what I'm about to say may seem unkind. It has a tendency to sound chauvinistic to the average woman, and the result is many women object to this biblical mandate.

So when you look at the whole area of submission, it was Almighty God who made the husband the wife's authority. So you'll have to take up your protest with Him. It was God's decision that the man would have headship in the relationship—husbands and wives are just supposed to follow His orders.

When done properly, that is, according to God's Word, the interaction between submission and authority can be a well-executed plan that is a pleasure to observe. Perhaps an illustration will provide a deeper understanding and help to explain God's thought process. There is a picture of perfect submission that is reflected in the Bible, and it represents the divine relationship between a man and wife.

We learn from Scripture that a wife is supposed to reverence

When a Woman Loves a Man

her husband (Ephesians 5:33 KJV). The word "reverence" literally means "to bow down." Now get the biblical picture. The corresponding action for the husband is to show her love and honor by putting his wife on a pedestal. While she is elevated by the manner in which he treats her, the only way they can have a face-to-face rapport is if she voluntarily bows her head downward in his direction. When you envision this image you will see that it is a beautiful way to be in a marriage relationship.

With this picture in mind, it is evident that God does not want a wife to dominate her husband. Instead, He wants her to lovingly surrender to her husband's headship.

There is another crucial picture of biblical submission that applies here. Scripture also compares a wife's submission to the same kind of submission that the church is subject to under the authority of Christ (Ephesians 5:24). In other words, if you are a woman who loves the Lord, you must be willing to subject yourself under Christ's authority. Simultaneously, if you are also a wife, you should have no problem submitting to your husband's authority. For a woman, these two acts of submission go hand in hand.

Why is the wife's submission to her husband such a critical component of a godly marriage? The answer is signaled by Paul's statement in 1 Corinthians 11:8: "For man does not originate from woman, but woman from man." Submission has everything to do with the hierarchy of human creation and the purpose God chose for the man and the woman. The husband was created to be the head, and the wife was designed to voluntarily defer to her husband. Submission has nothing to do with superiority, or inferiority—it is God's design for orderly functioning.

MAKE HIM NUMBER ONE

When a woman loves a man, her submissive devotion to him can be measured in very real ways. Above all else, God expects his leadership to be paramount in her mind. For example, whenever she needs help, the first person a woman should consult with is her husband, not her best friend or pastor. To ask for advice indicates that you value the person's insight and that you have confidence in their ability to lead you in the right direction. Conversely, not seeking advice from your husband builds a wall of resistance and silence on his part that hinders further communication. You are saying by your actions that whoever you are talking to has more credibility than he does. You are saying that you don't trust him to have an answer that you can respect. The reality is that most of the time, you are quite certain that his answer will not be what you want to hear.

A man is especially sensitive to this kind of situation, particularly if his wife seeks counsel from another male figure. The strong desire to be the hero and the person who can bring resolution to any problem or predicament is built into the psyche of a man.

Every man needs to know that his influence is powerful and vital to the woman in his life. Men are wired to fix things, to make things better. When you seek another man's advice you are denying your husband the chance to participate in whatever is going on and to make a meaningful contribution. You are letting him know that you don't appreciate how he takes care of things and there is someone who is better at it. That's not how you treat someone you respect.

Think of it this way: When you look for direction from anyone other than your husband, you indirectly communicate to him that he isn't man enough for you! On the other hand, inviting him to help with your daily decisions gives him frequent opportunities to be the hero in your life.

It is a husband's primary responsibility to maintain the well-being of his family. In support of his efforts to excel in his role, a godly wife will make it a well-known fact that her allegiance to her husband is her first priority. When a woman loves a man, she will appreciate his masculinity and convey her commitment to making him the primary relationship in her life.

MOVE OUT OF GOD'S WAY

Sadly, in the absence of this biblical mandate, there is an alternate way to conduct a marriage—and it's not so good. You're probably aware of it because it is prevalent among many married couples. With numerous Christian marriages ending in divorce, something is going very wrong.

From a wife's standpoint, at the root of the problem is often an unwillingness to submit. When submission is not practiced for whatever reason, there is wholesale dysfunction. If a woman feels like she cannot submit to her husband because she is dissatisfied with the way that he handles himself, you can bet there will be a lot of strife and bickering going on in that relationship.

This is one of the many reasons why God wants the wife to recognize her husband's headship. Almighty God knows how to mold even a difficult man into the man he was created to be. I didn't say it will be easy for her, but the sooner she gets in agreement with God and cooperates with God, the sooner the channel of blessings will begin to flow.

Most women want to see some form of positive change happen in their men. But the tendency is for a wife to try to effect that change on her own terms. Actually, if this sounds like your situation, let me tell you that it's counterproductive. When you get in the way, you stop God from dealing with your husband. Not only are you disregarding your husband, you are disregarding God. God is in the shaping, molding, conforming business—that's not your job. Nor is it your job to decide what kind of man he should be. Submit to the man you have and let God work. There is a saying

When a Woman Loves a Man

that says, "Step back and watch God move." There is a popular song that says, "Jesus will work it out if you let Him."

But the reverse is also true: When you move out of the way, you free up the hand of God to deal with your mate. So the best way to bring about an effective change, according to the Word of God, is to value your husband's authority. It is extremely unproductive to scratch and strain, trying to make him behave the way you want him to. Think about it. God doesn't force you to behave the way He wants you to behave, so what makes you think you can force your husband! Give him the honor that he's supposed to have, and let God do the rest.

When a woman loves a man, she appreciates who he is and what he does. God is trying to show you how to become a channel by which He can work in the life of your husband. It's so serious that, when you fail to do it God's way, you tie His hands. He can't work through you to bring about the positive changes you want to see in your husband. Don't worry; when you do it God's way, according to 1 Peter 3:1, God will cover you. He's got your back.

Moreover, what you need to understand is that this is an imperative. Remember, God's commandments are not optional. He is not asking you to submit. He's telling you this is what He expects of you. While God won't force you to submit, there are certain blessings you don't need to look for when you submit.

She Submits to His Headship

THE PROPER FIT

Just in case you're still wondering, the question is not, "*When* should I submit?" Or, "*How* should I submit?" If you are a wife, God intends you to submit to your husband at all times and in everything. Listen to what Paul wrote in Colossians 3:17–18,

> "Whatever you do in word or deed, do all in the name of the Lord Jesus, giving thanks through Him to God the Father. Wives, be subject to your husbands, as is fitting in the Lord."

Did you get that? He said, "Whatever you do." It's as simple as obeying God, but it seems to be a human tendency to make things complicated. All the while you're treating him like a king, remind yourself that you're doing it to please Jesus. Then go ahead and be bold enough to thank Him for giving you the grace to do it. Subject yourself to your husband's needs and expectations and watch God reward you for having the faith in Him to do something that you could not do without Him.

The word "fitting" means "proper, decent, and in order." I know that some of you are saying, "Well, wait a minute now. I've got some problems with this. My husband is not saved." Still others may ask, "What if I have a Christian man but he's not living a righteous life?" Guess what? The Word of God is not backing down. Submission is not just for Christian woman. Submission is for *all* women.

That's the trouble with today's culture. We want the right to disobey God but we don't want God to exercise His right to withhold blessings when we exercise that particular right. We're acting like we have the right to disobey God and decide for ourselves when we want to agree with God's principles. Most of the time we're not trying to be diligent about doing what is fitting in the Lord. We've violated God's order in the home. We've violated God's order in the church. And we've also violated God's order in society at large. It's a fact that many of the relationship problems people are experiencing are the result of the reversal of roles that is so common in these contemporary times.

Not unlike society in general, the Christian community is guilty as well of changing the definition of what it means to be a man. As I mentioned in my companion book, *When a Man Loves a Woman*, women have moved away from being appreciative of chivalry. Instead, they have chosen to become independent, "new-millennium" women. It is a shift from God's original plan that has caused a dilemma of sorts for many men because of the array of competing ideas as to who they should be. The collision between ideology and conflicting expectation has many men thoroughly confused about what they are supposed to do.

However, by no means is this something new. The problem stems from the beginning of humanity. Go back to the book of Genesis, chapter 3, and read the account that occurred just before the fall. Eve had her hand on her hip; talking to the devil—something she shouldn't have been doing in the first place.

When the Enemy approached her, she should have said, "Talk to my husband because when God gave him the word, I wasn't around." Instead, she stepped out of her role and her husband followed her lead. The combination of their missteps initiated the unleashing of the forces of darkness over the earth. And here we are dealing with the effects of their actions today.

Take a moment to look at some of the harsh portrayals of individuals who don't reflect the attributes of a virtuous woman. Unfortunately, these verses reveal a typical pattern of behavior going on in some marriages.

"It is better to live in a corner of a roof than in a house shared with a contentious woman." (Proverbs 21:9)
"A constant dripping on a day of steady rain and a contentious woman are alike." (Proverbs 27:15)

One preacher put it this way, "Whoa to the house where the hen crows louder than the rooster." Hmm.

RUNNING FOR COVER

To give us some insight into the thing that could drive a man away from one woman and into the arms of another, let's take a look

When a Woman Loves a Man

at the life of Samson. His story is found in the book of Judges, chapter 16. Although an Angel of the Lord visited Samson's parents before he was born and proclaimed that he was to live a special life as a Nazirite, Samson had a lot of issues when it came to women—he would pretty much love 'em and leave 'em—as they say.

For the most part, Samson lived a rebellious and carefree life, even to the point where he married a Philistine woman against his parents' wishes. The Bible says that he was attracted to her because she was pleasing to his eyes (Judges 14:3). That's another way to say that he wanted her because she was good looking. Mind you, her people, the Philistines were the archenemies of the Israelites at the time.

The Bible doesn't even tell us how that marriage fared. But it does say that he moved on. In his next escapades, which were mentioned in Judges 16:1, we can only imagine why he would hook up with Philistine prostitutes.

However, there is something curious about him that caught my attention. I wondered why Samson hooked up with Delilah. She was another Philistine woman, but the Bible never says Delilah was pretty. More than likely, we would have been informed in a similar way to the descriptions of other women of the Bible who were considered strikingly beautiful. For example, Rebekah's beauty was described in Genesis 24:16 (KJV); she was described as very fair.

But what about Delilah? My inquisitiveness led me on a search through the Scriptures because I wanted to know what in the world was going on in that relationship. What made Samson want to be with her?

Here is what I found. It wasn't her beauty and it wasn't her body. The text says that Samson would go to Delilah's house, put his head in her lap, and she would stroke his hair. That was it; the brother found some peace at this woman's house.

Do you know that most affairs are not about sex or beauty? Do you ever wonder what in the world would possess a man to be unfaithful to his wife? How many times has a man had an affair and people have made the comment, "He cheated on his wife with *her*"? It's not about the looks.

Please don't misunderstand me. I'm not giving anybody an excuse. When we sin, we are wrong—there are no two ways about it. Rather, I'm submitting to you a possible reason for infidelity that bears consideration.

In Samson's case, every time he was in Israel, they were pulling on him. He constantly had to fight against the Philistines. But at the end of the day, there seemed to be only one place where he could go and lay his head down and rest. In reality, Samson proved that it takes more than lips, hips, and fingertips to soothe a man's pain. And Delilah became a fountain of refreshment and restoration for him. He actually felt comfortable enough to come and lay his head in her lap. He didn't feel like he had to be on the defense, on guard for the next attack.

　　　　　　　　　　　　　　When a Woman Loves a Man

This is my point. The Bible says a man needs that kind of consolation from his wife. Otherwise, he may find it elsewhere.

AVOIDING A DEADLY TRAP

Now understand the context of this statement. I don't want anybody to think that I approve of affairs. It is my firm position that it is not a wife's fault if her husband has an extramarital affair. Furthermore, she should never allow him to put that blame on her. I'm also not talking about something that I read in a book. It's been my own experience as well. So I'm not picking on anyone.

I just want wives to be aware of the other side of the coin. The fact is that most affairs don't start out about sex. Someone may be asking, "Well, what is it all about? What does he see in the other woman?" Certainly, any woman with a husband who has had the misfortune of falling prey to an affair would want to know why. In many cases the other woman is not as attractive as the man's wife, and it's a difficult thing to comprehend.

Well, sometimes it's not about how she looked or what she had to offer—it's how she made him feel. That is the reality. Furthermore, a lack of submission on a wife's part can be the origin of the problems in a relationship. That is not to say it is the only thing that can be wrong, but submission is at the very core of a marriage. It's a fact, and it cannot be denied.

When a marriage is suffering from a deficiency of submission, the results can play out in so many troublesome ways. To illustrate my point, consider this scenario. Not only is it a common theme in television sitcoms, it happens in real life too.

The husband comes home to his wife wearing a tent masquerading as a dress and flip-flop shoes with a scarf wrapped around her head.

After a long day at the office, he asks, "Is dinner ready?" This is her response, "It'll be ready when you go out and buy some." After watching soap operas and reality shows most of the day, she then complains to him about the children. She's tired and wants him to spend some time with them.

The next day he goes to the office after an evening like this. One of the young ladies notices that he's down and asks, "What's wrong?"

He sighs and responds, "Oh, nothing . . . nothing." But she's already sensed that something is wrong and wants to cheer him up. She begins to tell him how much he's valued around the office.

"I am?" he says.

She responds, "Yes, we're really glad you're here. But we don't like to see you depressed. We're concerned about you."

At first he's reluctant to share his problems, but suddenly he opens up to her. The more he talks, the more he realizes that finally someone wants to hear what he has to say for a change. Someone who appears to be interested in him and his thoughts.

When a Woman Loves a Man

Most of the time he just listens, but now he has a chance to talk. So he says, "Well, you know, it's personal, but my wife's just been on me a little lately. She says I don't do this and I don't do that."

The young lady looks sincere and compassionate. She asks, "What's wrong with that girlfriend? Now, I'm not trying to come on to you, but all the ladies around here say that you're a really nice guy. I want you to know that I really appreciate you. I've been watching how you do your work. I think you're really going to move up in this company."

The next morning he finds a beautiful card on his desk. He hasn't seen one in a long time. It reads: *You are special. Just wanted you to know somebody cares.* When he opens it up to see who signed it, he catches a scent of perfume. Something he hasn't enjoyed in a long time. It simply says, *Y.K.W. (you know who).*

Now, true enough, it doesn't always happen this way, but many times that's the way affairs begin.

Generally speaking, men are exposed to ladies in the workplace who have pleasant personalities and are attractively dressed. They can't help but notice them. Furthermore, it can be a big turnoff after being in this environment all day only to return home to a nagging wife who complains about how tired she is—especially if she hasn't even cooked dinner. This kind of situation becomes increasingly volatile. Then the next thing he knows, one of the ladies makes him an offer: "Can I treat you to lunch?"

Now don't misunderstand me. I'm not blaming the wife for a man's sin. I'm trying to give women a little insight into the fact that affairs don't always start off with sex. They don't start with the intention of being anything. A man is being treated as someone of value, and he likes it and decides he wants more of it. You decide. Which do you think is most appealing—a constantly nagging wife or an attractive woman who has a listening ear?

THE DANGER ZONE

Whatever you do, dear ladies, beware of self-deception. According to God's Word in Ephesians 5, 1 Peter 3, and Colossians 3, a woman who is not in submission to her husband—no matter how spiritual she thinks she may be (she actually isn't spiritual)—is not in submission to the Lord. That's what the Bible says. As long as the man is not asking her to do anything that would violate God's Word, she must act in deference to her husband. Nine times out of ten the man is not asking her to do anything unbiblical. It may be uncomfortable, or even unpleasant, but not unbiblical. Otherwise, she is not in submission to Christ.

Maybe it's time to examine your own marriage relationship. You might find that you're not as spiritual as you think you are.

Here's an example to consider. As I travel along the highway, I cannot help but notice the signs posted indicating a speed limit of 30 miles per hour. Now I must admit that sometimes my right

When a Woman Loves a Man

foot doesn't act like it's saved. Somehow it loses its salvation and I find myself going over the speed limit. But I do understand that the sign is there for a reason. It is an indication of the state highway laws. When I don't submit and consequently break the traffic laws, I cannot say that I am a good citizen of the state. Am I correct? Nor can I blame the state for my disobedience.

In reference to God's designated chain of authority, think of your husband as the road sign. The state represents the Lord Jesus Christ. If you do not submit to your husband, you are not only in violation of his God-given authority, you are also violating the higher authority—the commandment of the Lord. And there are consequences.

GROUNDS FOR DIVORCE

I believe that Gloria Steinem, long-time activist and feminist, put it best. She said and I quote, "We women have finally become the man we wanted to marry." That may explain why so many are miserable.

Allow me to let you in on a well-kept secret, and please understand that I'm not trying to be cruel or harsh. It's tight, but it's right, and here it is: Some women can't live with their husbands because they refuse to get a divorce from themselves. Moreover, having a self-absorbed disposition is a direct contradiction to the characteristics of a virtuous woman. Instead of reflecting the traits of a godly woman, a woman who falls into the former category demonstrates an attitude that doesn't lend itself to building the solid foundation that is required for a strong marriage.

It may not be too popular to talk about it but, at the very crux of this problem, there is a resistance on behalf of some women to surrender control over their lives to another human being. What all wives and potential wives need to understand is that there must be a separation between their old lives and the new. The formula for success requires a whole lot of sacrifice and compromise—saturated with an unconditional love.

It's highly unfortunate that some women have a misunderstanding of the truth about what marriage is all about. Nevertheless, God expects wives to relinquish the control they once had as singles to their husbands so that He can bless marriages in the way He intends to.

That's why the severing of a marriage is a real tragedy because it doesn't represent God's way. When a woman loves a man, there is a fundamental need to keep herself aligned with the One who designed her. The more she guards her relationship with the Heavenly Father, the more it will enable her to do her part in the marriage. To that end, a wise and virtuous-minded woman will make this Scripture a part of her everyday life,

"To this end also we pray for you always, that our God will

count you worthy of your calling, and fulfill every desire for goodness and the work of faith with power, so that the name of our Lord Jesus will be glorified in you, and you in Him, according to the grace of our God and the Lord Jesus Christ." (2 Thessalonians 1:11–12)

There is nothing more powerful and precious than the prayers we find in the Scriptures, for they come directly from the inspiration of the Holy Spirit, who knows what we need and how to pray for us. If you want to keep your focus on your marriage and protect it from the threat of divorce, let the words of this prayer come to life for you.

Allow me to give you some further insight on the state of divorce. Here is an illustration of something you need to know. By the way, the reason I offer so many illustrations is because God has given us a wealth of pictures concerning the life He created for us. They can provide an invaluable resource tool to help us get to know the Lord better. So here's the biblical approach to dealing with divorce.

During the time of Jesus' ministry, there was an ongoing debate between two schools of thought on the subject of divorce. The question on the floor was: "Can a man divorce his wife for any reason?" On one side of the debate was Rabbi Hillel, and on the other Rabbi Shammai was standing his ground.

Rabbi Hillel represented the liberal perspective and contended that a man could divorce his wife for just about any reason at all. According to his reasoning, a man had sufficient grounds for divorce if his wife did any of the following:

- burned his dinner
- put too much salt on his dinner
- spun around in the street and showed her knees
- took her hair down without his permission
- spoke to a man in public
- spoke unkindly about his mother
- raised her voice loud enough to be heard on the other side of a wall

Undoubtedly, Rabbi Hillel would have a huge problem with the freedom women have to express themselves today. He might rethink his position if he were alive today. But these are the ideas he promoted. Besides, most men of his time were in agreement with him and were quick to rid themselves of their wives. Some men seem to hold this view even if they don't know were it came from. I suggest that even now, some men might still agree with Hillel.

In contrast, there was a completely different opinion as well. Rabbi Shammai held the position that a man could only divorce his wife over issues of immorality.

When Jesus came on the scene in Matthew, chapter 19, He didn't take either side. Someone asked His opinion, and this was His response:

"Have you not read that He who created them from the beginning made them male and female, and said, 'For this reason a man shall leave his father and mother and be joined to his wife, and the two shall become one flesh'? So they are no longer two, but one flesh. What therefore God has joined together, let no man separate." (Matthew 19:4–6)

Jesus was the most excellent teacher who ever walked this earth. He didn't give them a mere opinion; He settled the dispute by pointing them to the source of all wisdom and truth—the Word of God. The first thing He said to them was, "Have you not read?" His question was simple yet powerful. His message was profound. If the people wanted to know about divorce, they were not to take counsel from the likes of Hillel or Shammai; they should go directly to the divine blueprint on all marriage-related issues.

Here Jesus was setting the ultimate example for them. If you want to know how marriage ought to be and the acceptable grounds for dissolving a marital union—don't talk to any man. Consult the Divine Designer of the marriage institution. He took them back to the foundation to resolve the debate because no man can argue with the Word of God (that is, and win).

Because He is perfection, God designed the perfect institution for marriage. It's when the human element enters the picture that things go haywire. But not to worry, the Bible is here to keep us on the right track and hold us back from the bottomless abyss of hopelessness that can lead a couple to divorce.

The answer that the people of ancient times needed is recorded in the book of Genesis, and it is there for us too. Jesus said to go back to the divine blueprint and find out what God said. And so this is a message for all of us today—whether before you marry or after you marry—know what the Word of God has to say on the subject. And take care that you are rightly dividing the Word. Study it, meditate on it, listen to what God is saying while you read it so that you come away with what God says and not what you have twisted Scripture to mean. You'll put yourself in a better position to have a healthy, happy, godly marriage. And that's the kind God designed you to have.

WALK THE TALK

One preacher said he'd rather see a sermon on marriage than hear one any day. He'd rather someone walk with him than merely show him the way. He said he could learn how to do it if someone let him see it done. He could watch another's hands in action, but their tongue may run too fast. Finally, the lectures one delivers may be very wise and true, but he'd rather get his lesson by observing what that person does.

I agree wholeheartedly with these statements. For I may not understand you and the high advice you give, but there's no misunderstanding when I see how you act and how you live.

Your marriage relationship has the potential to be a living epistle from which others could watch and learn. In actuality, there are five gospels. Because some people will never read Matthew, Mark, Luke, and John, what good news can they gain from the gospel according to you? If you don't believe this, think about where many of your morals, opinions, life views came from. What do you remember most—what you heard or what you saw?

TWO WRONGS DON'T MAKE IT RIGHT

You say that you love the Lord. If submission is causing you great concern, perhaps you need some encouragement from some of the sisterhood. Recall the story of Hannah in the book of 1 Samuel. Consider how she submitted to her husband under less than ideal circumstances. Hannah didn't let anything stand in the way of her faith in God—not even her husband's disobedience.

You see, although it involved her husband, she needed something that only God could give her. The thing she longed for most in life was to have a child. But it took diligent faith and long-suffering before she eventually received her blessing. The Bible says that she rejoiced in the Lord's salvation (1 Samuel 2:1) because the Lord heard her petition and answered her.

Hannah was married to a man named Elkanah, who just happened to have two wives. It's no wonder that his name meant "grace is available." Having two wives, he needed that grace.

Now Hannah was his first wife, and his second wife was Peninnah. As you follow the story, Hannah is seen as a woman who is being disrespected by the second wife. She is in this situation due to the sin her husband incurred by marrying two women. With such tragedy plaguing her life, it was revealed in 1 Samuel 1:6 that Hannah is barren. To her further chagrin, Peninnah had several children and was giving her some serious "baby mama drama." Peninnah took every occasion to flaunt the fact that she had produced offspring for the husband they shared and Hannah could not.

But don't miss this integral part of the story. Scripture does not indicate that Hannah gave her husband any grief as a result of her distress. She could have said, "You've got this other wife and she's taunting me because I don't have any children." She could have given the both of them a lot of drama. Instead, notice what she does. She submitted to her husband even though he was in the wrong. Also notice that she truly submitted. Submission is not

When a Woman Loves a Man

doing what your husband asks you to do and then reminding him that you are submitting to him. Hannah didn't throw in his face that he was wrong and should only have one wife. She didn't call her girl-friends together to discuss how low down Elkanah was and what a tramp Peninnah was. She didn't bad mouth either one of them. She submitted to him without advertising that she was submitting. She wasn't looking for a woman of the year award because she was submitting even though she was getting the short end of the stick. Finally, because of her obedience to His Word, God fulfilled her utmost desire—to have a child.

DOING IT GOD'S WAY

The apostle Peter had some words of wisdom for wives (and aspiring wives) that, if taken to heart and applied diligently, could help keep a woman on track for the kind of wife who pleases God:

"In the same way, you wives, be submissive to your own husbands so that even if any of them are disobedient to the word, they may be won without a word by the behavior of their wives, as they observe your chaste and respectful behavior. Your adornment must not be merely external—braiding the hair, and wearing gold jewelry, or putting on dresses; but let it be the hidden person of the heart, with the imperishable quality of a gentle and quiet spirit, which is precious in the sight of God. For in this way in former times the holy women also, who hoped in God, used to adorn themselves, being submissive to their own husbands; just as Sarah obeyed Abraham, calling him lord, and you have become her children if you do what is right without being frightened by any fear." (1 Peter 3:1–6)

This is a divine prescription of the way in which a wife should honor and revere her husband—whether he is saved or not. I want to first point out something because I don't want to trip anyone up. In verse 3, Peter wasn't implying that a woman should neglect her personal appearance; he was emphasizing that outward beauty alone is not enough. Remember what we talked about earlier; no man wants to come home to a wife who looks like a bag lady. Put on some lipstick, a little eye-liner or mascara. Comb your hair and be dressed in something you wouldn't be ashamed to wear outside.

Rather, it is what's inside a woman's heart that matters. He went on to hold up the women of antiquity as an example. Not only did they hope in God, they also adorned themselves outwardly. So it wasn't about how they looked. Here is what made them pleasing to God—they submitted to their husbands.

Out of subjection, the Word of God says that the women of old called their husbands "lord," which meant "sir" or "master." For example, out of great respect for him, Sarah called Abraham "lord,"

When a Woman Loves a Man

(Genesis 18:12). Even though at times he did some questionable things in reference to his marriage, she maintained a proper esteem for her husband. Sarah did not allow Abraham's behavior to deter her from doing the right thing. Her faith in God gave her the strength to submit to him.

Note that it probably wasn't any easier for Sarah to subject herself to Abraham any more than it is a piece of cake for a woman today to do the same thing. Yet there is confirmation from Scripture that Sarah was rewarded for the way in which she conducted herself as a faithful and virtuous wife.

> "By faith even Sarah herself received ability to conceive, even beyond the proper time of life, since she considered Him faithful who had promised." (Hebrews 11:11)

Connect the dots for yourself. When Sarah heard the promise God gave her, she believed that God was faithful. As a result, she trusted Him and submitted herself to her husband because she knew it was the right thing to do. It may have taken a long time, but Sarah did what God expected of her and God fulfilled His promise. Against all odds, He gave her the long-awaited child—Isaac (Genesis 21:1–7).

Do you see what happened here? Some of you ladies need to understand this and apply it to your lives. The reason why God hasn't worked a miracle in your marriage yet, the reason God hasn't stepped in and worked on your man yet, is because you haven't submitted to your husband's authority. Instead of submitting you are trying to manipulate him and get him to do things your way. Or you are tearing him down not only verbally but by your actions as well. You need to remember that submission cannot be superficial. God looks directly at the heart.

Until He sees that you acknowledge your husband's leadership, you have tied the hand of God in giving you the blessing of any change that you so desire in your mate. Don't be deceived and fall into the trap of trying to do God's job rather than allowing Him to change your husband—something that is impossible for you to do anyway. Beware of trying to be God's assistant in husband-changing tasks—He doesn't need your help. He created the entire universe without you, so He can definitely change a husband without help. You just submit and do the things you are called to do and see the miracles that God will work on your behalf.

There is too much at stake here because your marriage is precious in God's sight. Stop trying to bless yourself. If you want the right results, you have to do it God's way. When you line up with God, then and only then will the proper channels of authority open up so that God's blessings will begin to flow to you and through you.

Of course, every woman's issue does not involve waiting on the

When a Woman Loves a Man

Lord to bless them in the way that Sarah hoped He would do for her. But because there are no perfect marriages, every wife has a desire for her marital relationship that she longs for the Lord to fulfill.

Now listen, I know what you're saying. "You've got to be out of your mind if you think I'm going to put up with anything and let God change my husband whenever He gets ready to." Change your thinking on this and get God's perspective. You are not putting up with anything; rather, you are honoring God. Remember Paul tells us in Colossians that everything we do is to be done as unto the Lord. That includes submitting to your husband. But, I'm saying this to you: The Word of God commands the wife's submission to her mate. And the only way that a woman can satisfy God's expectation is by surrendering herself to the power of God.

Subject yourself to Christ first, with your husband second only to Him. On the authority and integrity of the Word, it is the fitting, proper, decent, and orderly thing to do. And, believe me, when you do your part, you can count on God to do the rest.

As a final note, I want to quote Pastor Tony Evans here because I agree with him wholeheartedly. Some women need to go home and confess like this to their husbands: "Honey, I want to ask for your forgiveness. I have let my disagreements with you turn into disrespect for you. And for that disrespect to you, I am wrong. I want to begin today to recognize your leadership position that was given to you by God for this house, my lord."

You see, when a woman loves a man, she makes him feel like God intended for him to feel. She submits to his leadership. Not only does she accept and appreciate who he is, but she accepts and appreciates what he does. Try that and do like Sarah. Call him "lord," and let God deal with his faults. Just get out of the way and ask God to empower you. Then you'll begin to see what the Lord will do to bless your marriage.

Think *about it:*

1. What are some of the reasons women have a difficult time submitting to their husbands?

2. Does the analogy of the Trinity to the marriage relationship make it easier to understand your role as a wife? Why or why not?

3. In your personal relationship, how do you avoid the lines between your and your husband's roles being crossed?

4. Do you have disagreements over the various ways that your marriage functions?

5. Do the two of you have healthy discussions that facilitate you in carrying out your respective roles?

Live *by it:*

Dear Heavenly Father, I ask You to preserve the marriage of every woman who desires to please You by being a virtuous wife. Help them to understand that Your mandate of submission is designed to bless their lives. According to Your divine design, show each woman how to submit to her husband's headship as she ultimately submits to You, in Christ's name. So be it.

cherish is the word

when a woman loves *a man,* she cherishes him

A WOMAN WENT with her husband for his annual physical checkup. The doctor performed the usual tests: checked his blood pressure, took some blood, listened to his heart, and examined his throat and ears. The man could see the concern on the doctor's face, but the doctor didn't say anything to him after he finished the examination.

While the man was getting dressed, the doctor asked the wife if he could speak with her.

The doctor furrowed his brow and in a somber manner he asked her, "Do you love your husband?"

She answered, "Oh yes, I certainly do."

"Very well," he said. "I need to let you know that unless you do the following things for him, your husband is going to die very soon."

The woman was visibly stunned. With a serious tone, she responded, "Well, what should I do? Tell me, because I need to know. I love him and I don't want him to die."

The doctor replied, "Okay. This is what you must do. Every morning he's got to have a hot breakfast. It must not be cold cereal and milk. It has to be eggs and bacon, or sausage, with biscuits, grits, and home fries. It's really critical that he have this every day. In addition, you must insist that he come home for lunch. He cannot have a sandwich from a fast-food place. You have to lay it out and do everything from scratch so that he has a healthy meal with all the nutrients that he needs."

The doctor wasn't finished yet. He went on, "For dinner, never serve him anything prepared in a microwave oven. Everything that he eats must be fresh; none of the ingredients should come from a can or out of a box. Make sure each meal contains all of the food groups. I cannot stress this enough. You've got to take exceptionally good care of him. And let me just add that he's also very susceptible to germs, so don't allow him to be around any garbage whatsoever. Furthermore, you'll have to dust and keep the house immaculately clean because dust contains harmful germs. That means you'll need to dust at least two or three times a week. Keep everything extremely clean."

Finally, he completed his instructions and the wife said, "Yes, doctor. I understand."

On the way home, the husband said to her, "I saw you talking to the doctor. What did he say?"

Sadly, she replied, "He said you're going to die."

CHERISH IS THE WORD

You see, this woman's problem was that she professed love but wasn't prepared to back it up with her actions. She failed to realize that you can give without loving, but you can't demonstrate love without giving. This misguided wife claimed that she loved her husband but, when the rubber met the road, it was obvious from her own words that love wasn't forthcoming. Putting it concisely, she reacted selfishly to his dilemma.

What was her problem? I like to say it this way: the milk of human kindness had curdled within her. In fact, it had definitely spoiled. There is a word that was missing from her vocabulary, and consequently, it wasn't manifested in her behavior. That word is "cherish." Webster's definition of cherish is "to keep or cultivate with care and affection." Based on its meaning, to cherish someone is the exact opposite of acting out of selfish motives.

Truthfully speaking, a wife may act selfishly toward her

husband without even being aware of how it comes across. This will happen if, before she takes her wedding vows, a critical transition has not taken place in her psyche to help her switch from thinking as a single person to behaving as a godly wife.

A key component of her preparation for marriage will distinguish her mentality as a single woman from the mind-set that will cause her to become a virtuous wife. That component involves her relationship with God. The more a woman is committed to the Lord, the more she will be devoted to making her marriage work according to God's design.

Now I do realize that what I'm about to say may sound harsh. So please know that this is not *my* message to you; I am only the messenger. According to the Bible, there are two opposite approaches to take on the role of being a wife. Scripture says that a woman can either be a crown on her husband's head or a cancer eating away at his life.

The Word of God alone has the authority to draw the distinction between these two conflicting choices for a wife. Here it is straight from God's Word: "An excellent wife is the crown of her husband, but she who shames him is like rottenness in his bones" (Proverbs 12:4).

This is a stark reality, but it's also true and forever settled in heaven. So, from which of these realities do you think a husband would benefit and prefer? A wife can be a healer or a hell-raiser. She can give compliments or complaints. She can be a nurturer or a nagger. She can be a helper or a hinderer.

God attaches great significance to the wife who places herself as a crown upon her husband. And we know crowns are worn proudly. You may wonder why your husband doesn't seem appreciative of you and what you do. Take a look at what Scripture says and evaluate yourself to see if you are giving him anything to appreciate. In light of what is at risk—a marriage that pleases God—my prayer is for every wife to aim toward God's plan for her. And the only way a woman can be a crown for her husband is when she diligently pursues the traits of a virtuous woman. Ultimately, her inclination will grow out of a knowledge and willingness to make her marriage reflect the godly union that God would have it to be.

As a result of her efforts, when a woman loves a man, she cherishes him and makes him feel like a king. And if a man is going to feel like a king, it's only because the woman he marries is his crown. That is the job of a wife—to give her husband his proper place.

For every wife, there's a simple way to test whether her relationship measures up. Perform routine checkups on how you consider his needs. Do you treat him like a king or a pauper—because he's only king if you crown him so.

HE'S THE MAN

What does it look like when a woman places herself as a crown on her husband's head? It is observed through the loving ways that she cherishes him. A wife who crowns her husband demonstrates deep affection through her behavior and attitude toward him.

Therefore, when a woman loves a man, there are two key ways that she shows him:

1. She cherishes him by reverencing his position.
2. She cherishes him by respecting his person.

Although sometimes "reverence" and "respect" are used interchangeably, there is a difference in their meaning. In reverence, a wife is concerned about his position. And out of respect for him, she is concerned about his person. When these two elements come together, a husband cannot help but know that she highly regards and cherishes him.

IN ALL YOUR GETTING, GET UNDERSTANDING

Since this is all about God's perspective on the role of a wife, you may be wondering, "How do you know when a woman loves a man?" If you are, then you're ready to learn more about understanding what God expects of you as a wife. So then we must take the first step in exploring what it means to cherish a man by giving him reverence and respect.

Moreover, I've got good news because Scripture has provided all the knowledge needed on this subject. I'm a firm believer that there's no better way in which to gain an understanding than to study real examples, so let's go directly to the Bible.

There is a beautiful story that depicts the process that unfolds when a woman loves a man. It is found in the book of Ruth. I would encourage anyone to read the entire book of Ruth to gain insight into the deep spiritual meaning that is found there. Not only does it give us a profound picture of the kind of relationship God desires between a man and a woman, it reveals the unconditional love of God and redemption that He provided for His people.

Let me give you a brief background on what transpired. Ruth was a woman from the country of Moab who met and married a man from Bethlehem. The man had moved to Ruth's homeland with his father, mother, and brother because there was a famine in Israel. While they were in Moab, the three men perished, which left the women to fend for themselves. Looking forward to the challenges of the future, it became a time of decision.

The young widow, Ruth, decided to follow her mother-in-law, Naomi, back to Israel. In spite of Naomi's urging her to stay in her own hometown, Ruth had made up her mind. Unlike her sister-in-law, Orpah, it doesn't even appear that she contemplated taking the easy choice to remain in the familiar surroundings of her homeland.

Ruth being a woman with strong character and loyalty, the Bible says that she clung to Naomi. Apparently Ruth didn't have a monster-in-law for a mother-in-law. This suggests that because she reverenced and respected her husband she had no problem watching out for his mother. The verse most people are familiar with is that of her saying to Naomi,

> "Do not urge me to leave you or turn back from following you; for where you go, I will go, and where you lodge, I will lodge. Your people shall be my people, and your God, my God." (Ruth 1:16)

These two women were in dire straits. In those days women weren't liberated according to today's standards. Naomi was an older woman with virtually no chance to remarry. More than likely she would have to accept whatever life she could manage to mete out. Without a husband, Ruth had no representative. A widowed woman like herself needed the covering of a man. Therefore, to protect her from being vulnerable in society, she needed someone to redeem her.

Beyond a doubt, Ruth had some challenges to overcome. She was not of the household of Israel. In fact, she wasn't allowed to enter a Jewish temple. That means she couldn't even go to church—the one place it is believed a single person can find a good mate.

When a Woman Loves a Man

Furthermore, it was uncommon for the people of Israel to marry outside of their faith.

So here we get a glimpse of her loyalty to Naomi. Ruth would have to endure the fact that, as a foreign woman, she would not be fully embraced. However, God provided her saving grace. If she was to have any chance at remarrying, Ruth would need her deceased husband's relative—a kinsman-redeemer—to marry and provide for her.

And God did not disappoint her. He provided a kinsman-redeemer who had the ability to take her from being an outcast and place her in the family of God. Now, we know this is a picture of the Lord Jesus Christ because He did the same thing for us. Jesus is our Kinsman-Redeemer who came to earth as a near relative and purchased back everything we lost after Adam's fall from grace, including our right to fellowship with God.

This story clearly expresses how God was in control throughout the lives of Ruth and Naomi. He orchestrated events and made available to Ruth a man named Boaz. As was the custom of the culture, if he chose to, he would be able to provide the security that Ruth needed so much.

First of all, Boaz was a relative of Naomi's. He also happened to be a wealthy man. Boaz was obviously a bachelor because the Bible did not mention anything about him having a wife. So in this passage Naomi is instructing Ruth on how to be a crown on his head and treat Boaz like a king, according to God's design.

Naomi actually schooled her in the way described in the book of Titus, chapter 2, which we covered earlier. As a mature woman, it was her role to teach Ruth how to introduce herself to this good man. Listen to her wisdom and experience evident as she began to instruct her daughter-in-law:

"Wash yourself therefore, and anoint yourself and put on your best clothes, and go down to the threshing floor; but do not make yourself known to the man until he has finished eating and drinking. It shall be when he lies down, that you shall notice the place where he lies, and you shall go and uncover his feet and lie down; then he will tell you what you shall do." She said to her, "All that you say I will do." (Ruth 3:3–5)

I must pause here to explain the context of this passage because at first glance it sounds as if Naomi is teaching Ruth how to simply catch a man. But you have to know something about the culture of the time to understand what's going on here. If Ruth had even a brother or some other male figure to speak for her, he could have spoken to Boaz on her behalf.

But there was no other man in Ruth's life. So don't miss this or you'll make the wrong assumption about the two women's motives. They weren't trying to do something underhanded to set up some man. They weren't following *Cosmopolitan*'s "10 Ways to Catch a Man."

It is understood that Naomi was teaching Ruth the proper etiquette and manner for making an appeal to a kinsman-redeemer. Everything these women did was aboveboard.

PREPARATION IS KEY

In fact, if you study the instructions that Naomi gave to Ruth, you will find some timeless and fundamental principles that are appropriate for godly women today who want to teach their daughters how to prepare for marriage.

But unfortunately, this is a sticking point for many women today. They weren't prepared for submission to headship and obedience to the man that God placed over them. They might have thought they were fully prepared only to find out later that they weren't as prepared as they should be. As a result, many women enter into marriage in self-deception about what God expects of them as a wife.

At the wedding ceremony when the couple was presented as "Mr. and Mrs.," along with the man's last name, they didn't realize this was an acknowledgement from the woman that she would do in her life what she had just done with her last name. In effect, she was saying, "I will switch authority—from my father to my husband—and this man shall be my covenant head from now on."

If you're single and you're not prepared to do that, it's better that you not get married. I'm telling you it will be difficult to endure the test of time because a man needs to be king in his castle and the crown on his head is his wife. That is the way God designed marriage to be.

Reverence His Position, Step 1

Scripture says that the wife must see to it that she reverence her husband (Ephesians 5:33 KJV). In other passages, the word "reverence" is used for worshipping God. It's the same word. But by no means does this suggest that a woman must worship her husband. Worship is for God alone. Reverence his position in the household, but only worship the Lord. It does mean that the husband has a position that has been given to him by God—and it should be regarded as such. This position was given to him by God. He didn't wake up and decide he should be the head of his house—God decided that for him. It would be good for both parties to remember their positions and functions were decided by God.

It has to be highlighted that if a woman does not reverence her husband, she should not be deceived into thinking that she can give reverence to the Lord. Because there are both spiritual as well as physical aspects to this principle, not only should a woman develop a strong relationship with the Lord, she has to prepare herself physically. That is why Naomi said to Ruth, "Wash yourself therefore, and anoint yourself and put on your best clothes" (verse 3).

There is something very important about Ruth that every single woman should take note of. As a single lady, Ruth learned how to cherish a man *before* she married him. Through Naomi's guidance, she was prepared in such a way that she wouldn't have a problem giving him reverence and respect should they marry. This is the fundamental principle: Before you ever begin to think about a man, first learn how to present yourself. Clean hands go along with a pure heart and bring blessings from the Lord (Psalm 24:4–5).

Here was an older woman teaching a younger woman that before she could prove herself to a potential husband, she must first know how to care for herself. The intent of Ruth anointing herself with perfume was not to trap the man. Naomi didn't tell her to put on some White Diamond and her tight little black dress and go after him. No, it wasn't about that. Ruth was not a harlot; she was a virtuous woman. Out of reverence for the man of her interest, the perfume she put on would enhance her physical hygiene and make her presentable. The idea was that she could show Boaz that she was a respectable woman.

Now why did Naomi start there? She understood that a woman who wants to present herself to a man needs to let that man know something extremely important about her: she's a woman who knows how to take care of a man. In other words, the shower was not a foreign place to her. She was taught proper cleansing and hygiene.

For this very reason, there are a lot of people who aren't ready for a relationship with a man. They haven't learned how to first love and care for themselves. How can a woman love a man and she doesn't love herself? How can she take care of a man when she doesn't take care of herself? In fact, to tell us how important this practice is, Jesus gave us the second greatest commandment, "You shall love your neighbor as yourself" (Matthew 22:39).

Of course this commandment applies to every conceivable interaction between human beings. But when it comes to women, it includes the message of learning how to love yourself before you try to love someone else.

On the surface, it may sound trivial yet it has profound implications. Buy yourself some nice perfume and bubble bath and enjoy a soothing hot bath. Go out and buy a new outfit. Get your hair done. Put on some makeup. Take yourself out to dinner. Do these things solely because it is critical to your overall well-being that you love yourself first. You ought to get in the mirror and say, "Girlfriend, you know you got it going on."

Reverence His Position, Step 2

Ruth definitely got Boaz's attention. These next verses record their interaction. When Boaz inquired who she was, notice her response:

When a Woman Loves a Man

"He said, 'Who are you?' And she answered, 'I am Ruth your maid. So spread your covering over your maid, for you are a close relative.' . . . Then she fell on her face, bowing to the ground and said to him, 'Why have I found favor in your sight that you should take notice of me, since I am a foreigner?'" (Ruth 3:9; 2:10)

Here she is bowing at his feet out of reverence to his position. It was a sign of true submission on her part. Ruth's character showed great humility. It's an attractive and godly trait to possess—and it wasn't lost on Boaz.

The way in which their relationship developed makes sense if you understand that God has designed the man to be the head of the woman. Then it stands to reason that He has given men a position over women. If you find this too difficult to accept, it might help to keep it in the right perspective and remember that God made the woman for the man—and not the man for the woman (1 Corinthians 11:9).

The same principle and the truth of God's Word stand today. For that reason, in God's sight, the brothers are supposed to be in charge and the women are to follow their leadership. Furthermore, not only should men be leading in marriage, in the family, and in the church—men ought to be leading in society as a whole. In fact,

I need to point out another very important detail. Recall in 1 Corinthians 11:3, Paul said, "I want you to understand that Christ is the head of every man, and the man is the head of a woman, and God is the head of Christ."

If this instruction was intended for marriage partners only, the Word of God would have specifically noted that the head of the *wife* is the *husband*. But the principle is for all of society. That is why the Scripture purposely refers to "man" and "woman." In the social order, men were given headship authority by God—the One who created all things. If we want to consider the whole counsel of God, we have to take our direction from the One who is called Wonderful Counselor, Mighty God, Eternal Father, and the Prince of Peace (Isaiah 9:6).

Stay in Your Lane

I have discovered a recurring challenge to the male leadership role in general which stems from the dynamic between male and female interactions. When men and women don't give each other their due respect, it causes serious problems. The results are two-pronged: a lack of reverence for each other goes against the plan God designed for marriage and it also contributes to societal dysfunction in general.

Over my many years of counseling couples, I have reached the conclusion that the problem in some relationships comes down to a woman acting like a man's mother instead of his wife. As a result, the husband/wife relationship is replaced by a mother/son relationship. Let me say it this way: A woman can't be a man's mother and his lover at the same time. It's not possible and it is definitely not helpful.

Think about it. When the normal functions of a wife and a husband are distorted, the marriage will suffer. Moreover, the two partners have a shared responsibility in allowing their roles to be compromised. God's original plan was for the husband to support her by holding a job outside the home. The man was also given the authority to govern all matters that affect the family. The woman was to support him in his role by maintaining the home.

Typically, when a marriage does not function as God intended, the crux of the issue is that the husband has given up his leadership position. Naturally, someone has to take charge; otherwise there will be overwhelming chaos. The wife then steps into the leadership role and makes all the decisions. This situation more closely resembles a mother/son relationship where it is expected that a mother would assume an authoritative position.

Understand this: In a marital relationship, it is not that a wife's input is invalid or unnecessary, but her role should be her husband's primary advisor and not his supervisor. Although neither partner may be consciously aware of the adverse effect a role reversal may have, it tampers with the psychological aspects of the relationship. Most significantly, it shakes the spiritual foundation on which the marriage rests.

The Root of the Problem

God bases everything on divine principles. Therefore, if a wife defies her husband's position of headship, she is acting in disobedience to God. Someone once brought to my attention a critical piece of information. In regard to authority between a husband and wife, Scripture says Adam and Eve's eyes were opened after Adam ate (Genesis 3:6–7). When Eve ate, their eyes were still closed because she was not responsible for their actions. Remember, God commanded Adam not to eat of the tree of knowledge of good and evil (Genesis 2:17). As the representative head, Adam was held accountable.

Here's where the troubles of human existence all began. God gave Adam the word, His divine instructions, so that Adam could teach his wife. But when the woman disobeyed God's instructions, some very serious events unfolded. Adam and Eve were banished from fellowship with God. After He issued their discipline, their lives were changed forever. They were divested of God's bountiful provision and had to work for their sustenance by tilling the very same ground from which they had come.

How did this devolution begin? The problem was initiated when Eve violated the pattern that God established. Here we are in Genesis, chapter 3, and the serpent is talking to the woman. That conversation should have never occurred. Eve was supposed to call for her husband so that Adam could handle the situation. She knew that God had given him authority over their relationship. She should have told the serpent, "I wasn't there when God gave him the word. You come on and talk to him."

Instead, she spoke for herself. When she took matters into her own hands, she denied Adam the reverence that he was supposed to have. Later on, when the Lord God spoke to the woman, He said, "Your desire will be for your husband, and he will rule over you" (Genesis 3:16b).

This statement solidified the never-ending angst between the two genders. As part of her punishment, God was saying to Eve that from then on she would be inclined to dominate over Adam. At the same time, Adam wasn't excused either. From then on he would have a predisposition to act as a dictator over her. These issues still exist.

Here we find the perpetual root of relationship problems between wives and their husbands. Down through the annals of time it has become challenging to avoid this ongoing dilemma. To say the least, that is what makes the marriage relationship so delicate. The task for a woman who loves a man is to be very careful to show him deference and reverence. It's a dangerous thing to have the kind of attitude that says to her husband, "If I want your opinion, I'll give it to you."

Such a statement is an indication of what happens when the lines between the regard for his position and the dissatisfaction with his practice get confused. If you disagree with him in practice because he does something that you are opposed to, your reaction can easily turn into disregard for his position. You see, ladies, this is where the man's position of reverence gets compromised. Since knowledge is power, use this information to protect the way that you reverence your husband.

I know this can be a slippery slope, and it often comes down to those little irritating things a man does without giving it a second thought. Let me give you a quick example. Some men are challenged when it comes to tidiness and think nothing of leaving their clothing strewn about the house—wherever it may happen to fall.

When a wife is constantly vexed over this seemingly small issue, it can turn into a heated debate. Demeaning words are said that can't be taken back later. The moral of the story is, even if you don't approve of the man's cleanliness habits or something else about him that may irritate you, find a way to handle it so that it doesn't affect your reverence for his position.

Respect His Person

I think this is a pretty safe statement to make: men and women have different needs. In the marriage equation, a husband must esteem his wife. He is commanded to show her devoted TLC, or tender loving care. God unequivocally intends husbands to massage the emotions of their wives. The Bible addresses this crucial issue in Colossians 3:19: "Husbands, love your wives and do not be embittered against them."

Furthermore, Ephesians 5:25 says, "Husbands, love your wives, just as Christ also loved the church and gave Himself up for her." So here we have two admonitions regarding the husband's deeply abiding care for his wife. He is to be committed to her spiritual, emotional, and intellectual growth. Clearly, the man has been given a great responsibility to imitate our Lord's love for the church by loving his wife.

But a man doesn't need that kind of treatment. A man needs R-E-S-P-E-C-T. In fact, when a woman loves a man, she understands that the most important way to demonstrate love to her man is to show him respect. It is absolutely critical for women to understand how vital it is to a man's well-being to receive this type of acknowledgment and consideration. Men not only crave respect—they need it.

To find out more about the kind of respect that a man needs, we need to look at another cultural-related event that occurred in these next verses.

"So she went down to the threshing floor and did according to all that her mother-in-law had commanded her. When Boaz had eaten and drunk and his heart was merry, he went to lie down at the end of the heap of grain; and she came secretly, and uncovered his feet and lay down. It happened in the middle of the night that the man was startled and bent forward; and behold, a woman was lying at his feet." (Ruth 3:6–8)

The first thing we find here is Ruth following her mentor's instructions on proper protocol. Naomi sent her to his place of business, which was the threshing floor. Men slept there at night to protect their grain. Please take note that Naomi would have never sent Ruth to his house since that would be inappropriate. Ladies, be careful who you listen to; someone who has your best interest at heart will not tell you to do something inappropriate. However, it was appropriate for her to go to the threshing floor because that was like going to the city gates during the day.

By telling her not to make herself known to Boaz until he was finished eating, Naomi taught Ruth the meaning of being polite. The appropriate etiquette of the day was for the woman to wait. Ruth would have been out of line if she had walked up to Boaz saying, "Excuse me, but I need to see you right now."

Does this sound remotely familiar to anyone? I'm not suggesting that at all, but some young ladies today could learn from Ruth's example and demonstrate that they have been taught correct behavior. Yet, in this "everything goes" culture of today, an atti-

When a Woman Loves a Man

tude of disrespect has greatly overshadowed the rules that worked in the past.

As the story progresses, Boaz woke up in the middle of the night and found someone lying at his feet. It was Ruth, showing her respect. When she told Boaz who she was, Ruth politely added that she also knew who he was. Calling him, "a close relative," she endeared herself to him and recognized him as a person of authority.

In so many words, Naomi had said to her, "You go and tell him that you understand God has given us all a role." It wasn't that he was more powerful or superior than she; they just knew that in the relationship between a man and a woman, God has given the woman to be the follower of her man.

Ruth wanted a proper relationship with Boaz; that is, a husband/wife relationship. Not a mother/son relationship. She wasn't supposed to be his mother and his lover at the same time. By doing things the right way she demonstrated that she understood what her role was to be. She understood that he wasn't looking for a supervisor; he just needed somebody to be his chief adviser. She wanted him to know that she would follow him and let him lead the way.

NO IDENTITY CRISIS HERE

Now take note of this. In verse 9, Ruth identified herself as Boaz's servant by saying, "I am Ruth your maid." But something else very meaningful had taken place. In earlier chapters, Ruth was called "the Moabitess" (1:22; 2:21). The fact is, Ruth was her person and Moabite was her people. So in the beginning of her journey, she was identified with her people.

However, in chapter 3 verse 9, when she presented herself to Boaz, she took on a new identity. By faith (because it had yet to happen), Ruth said with reverential respect to Boaz that, if he would redeem her, she would become Ruth, his servant. With Boaz as her intended kinsman-redeemer, she was willing to no longer be known as Ruth, the Moabitess. By the grace of God, she called herself what she intended to become. In other words, she wasn't looking at herself with her past identity; instead, she looked forward to her future redemption. Ladies, if you want to be a godly wife, let go of the past. How you identified yourself in the past should stay in the past. You are now going to take on the identity of your husband. Before marriage, he has to know that you are willing to be identified with him.

Then, she said this: "Spread your covering over your maid," (verse 9). In the King James Bible the word "skirt," is used, which is translated as "wings." When Boaz spoke to her, he used this same word in Ruth 2:12 (KJV): "The Lord recompense thy work, and a full reward be given thee of the Lord God of Israel, under whose wings thou art come to trust."

The two of them were talking about some serious faith in this exchange. The word "wings" translated in Ruth 2:12 is the same word "skirt" translated in Ruth 3:9, and both refer to a covering. There is an important principle revealed here that applies to everyone. Ruth asked God to cover her before she asked the man to cover her. Ladies, be careful about asking a man to do for you what you should be asking God to do. Don't look to a man to meet your needs until you have gone to God.

In essence, here's what she was saying as she lie at Boaz's feet: "If you will cover me, I will respect your person and look to your provisions. I will become your possession." She made him an offer he could not refuse. I believe Boaz recognized her deep level of admiration and responded positively to her. A man in his position would be hard-pressed to deny a virtuous woman who highly esteems him. I will say it again: Men need respect.

LOOKING FOR MR. RIGHT

Let me tell you what Ruth knew that every single woman ought to know. Getting married is not about finding the person with whom you think you can live. Marriage is about finding the person that you can't live without; that is, the one God designed for you. Marriage is about being the right person; knowing who you are in Christ and what has been ordained for you. When these things are clearly understood it is easier to be what God wants you to be as a woman and as a wife.

Ruth clearly understood this. But, I know what some of you

are thinking: *I am not a weak, can't-do-anything-without-a-man kind of woman. This is wimpy stuff. I'm a strong woman. He wants some old weak kind of woman. I earned my promotions on my merits. I bought my own condo before I married him. I bought my own car. I've always dressed nice. I handle my finances very well and I know how to make decisions.*

I would not doubt a woman's ability to achieve those things on her own. Ruth may not have had all that going for her, but don't think for a minute that she was a wimp. It took courage and integrity to behave the way that she did. She was on a mission, so to speak, and was determined to do it God's way.

The other women attempted to ostracize her because she was different, but she stood her ground. She wasn't ashamed to pick herself up, go out into the field, and glean alongside the other women. I can imagine how they probably looked at her with disdain. "How did she get in here? Look at the way she's working. Who's she trying to impress? I don't have to work that hard. She's just Naomi's daughter-in-law. Why did she bring her here? I hope she doesn't think she's coming in here taking one of our men. She needs to go back where she came from. Nobody wants to be bothered with her."

But Ruth wasn't discouraged by her circumstances. It's true that they could have said whatever mean things they wanted to and treat her badly. However, they couldn't deny her tenacity. This was not a wimpy woman—this was a determined woman.

Now, for the ladies who are single, let me offer some insight here. If you're a strong woman, don't marry a wimpy man. Did you hear what I said? Get a man who's stronger than you. What do I mean by that? Get a man who won't be intimidated even if you make more money than he does. If you meet a man who doesn't have a degree and you have a Ph.D., make sure it won't bother him because he will still know that he is the man.

Of course there are some men who just happen to be quiet storms. They don't say a whole lot, but they take care of business. I'm not talking about that. I'm talking about somebody who is too timid to make a decision. For example, a teacher once asked her class, "What comes in like a lion and goes out like a lamb?" One boy answered, "My daddy."

If you're a strong woman, you don't want a man like that because contrary to what you think, you won't be able to make that man have a different personality than the one that God gave him. It won't be easy to submit to a man who lacks leadership capabilities.

Now let me share this prayer with you because I believe that it contains volumes of wisdom. It was spoken by a godly woman and it really bears repeating. Out of reverence and respect for her husband, she simply prayed: "Lord, give my husband the wisdom to lead and give me the grace to follow."

It reminds me of Proverbs 3:5–6: "Trust in the Lord with all your heart and do not lean on your own understanding. In all your ways acknowledge Him, and He will make your paths straight." If husbands and wives were to follow this principle, it would help women to keep silent so their men could hear from God and follow Him. Don't assume your husband isn't listening to God—make sure you aren't talking so much that he can't hear God. Without a doubt there would be so many more couples with successful marriages being led by God's Word.

Here is another example of the mind-set God wants a wife to have toward her husband. Once when a couple was joining our congregation, the wife stood up and said she wanted to join because God had led her husband to our church. She wasn't ashamed to admit that she follows her husband because that is what a wife is supposed to do.

WHEN A WOMAN LOVES A MAN: SHE CHERISHES, REVERENCES, AND RESPECTS HIM

She will do these critical things no matter what issues she and her husband are dealing with—including money. The bottom line is that a virtuous wife never loses her ability to treasure her husband. I contend if you study Ruth's life, a woman who was blessed beyond measure because she followed the plan of God, you will learn something that will improve your marriage. You will experience results you never expected as you diligently apply yourself and cherish your husband. Like Ruth, show him what it means to have a good woman and a good wife. Be the crown on your husband's head.

A wise woman will put her relationship in perspective. She will take the time to understand Proverbs 12:4 because she recognizes the value of helping her man to be successful. I guarantee you that, if a married man is doing well, his wife has made sacrifices and done her part to elevate him. If he's living his role as a king it's because she put the crown of herself upon his head. The successful man has a woman who reverences his position and respects his person. And it's not going to happen any other way.

I have one final comment for you. It doesn't matter whether you are the wife of a CEO (Chief Executive Officer) or a maintenance man. To be a virtuous woman, it takes the right attitude. Do you understand that you can help make your husband the man that God wants him to be? Not by trying to pressure him. Not by trying to push him. Not trying to shape and mold him. But by being the kind of woman that cherishes her mate for who he is.

Think *about it:*

1. Have you ever thought of yourself as a crown that your husband wears?

2. Do you understand the difference between giving without loving and loving with giving?

3. When you look in the mirror, do you see a selfish person or a giving person looking back at you?
4. How would you explain to an unmarried friend that a wife must be prepared to give reverence and respect to her husband?
5. Do you agree with the validity of the statement that some husband/wife relationships are replaced by a mother/son relationship? Have you ever witnessed such a relationship?

Live *by it*:

Dear Heavenly Father, we thank You for the teachings that You so graciously provide for those who want to be in Your will. Prepare every woman to be the virtuous woman that You have called her to be. By Your Holy Spirit, lead every wife in the proper way to cherish her mate. Out of reverence and respect for her husband, teach her how to submit so that she will please You in all her ways, in Christ's name. So be it.

Chapter Five
a tangible love

when a woman loves *a man,*
she cares for him

A MAN WAS lying on his deathbed, thinking about how he would soon be in the presence of the Lord. As he faded in and out of life, he noticed the smell of his favorite cookies. He thought, *Cookies, she's making cookies.* So he crawled out of the bed and down the stairs thinking about his favorite cookies. He continued to crawl through the living room and the dining room, heading for one last taste of those cookies.

When he finally reached the kitchen, there was his wife, taking a tray of cookies out of the oven. In a weak voice, he said the word, "cookies." And with one hand he reached up to grab his prize. To his surprise, his wife scolded him and said, "Put that down. They're for the funeral."

Now, that was really cold, wasn't it? Well, this story may be a little unlikely, but it really makes my point. It appears as though somewhere along the way this husband and wife lost the connection that binds marriage partners together.

Have you ever thought about what it means to love someone? I mean, *really* love someone. Not the kind of love you so often hear people casually talking about. They tend to throw the word around carelessly without even having a clue as to what genuine love is all about.

Thank God for His Word; it has the power to rescue us from ourselves. If the Holy Spirit had not inspired the apostle Paul to so eloquently describe the meaning of authentic love in 1 Corinthians, chapter 13, we wouldn't understand that God is the epitome of love. And we would have no other recourse but to wallow in a state of ignorant bliss instead of truly demonstrating our love to God and other people.

So when it comes to knowing what it's like for a woman to really love a man, I strongly believe there is so much more to learn about real love—God's kind of love. For that reason, it's necessary for me to turn once again to the divine blueprint. Discovering the meaning of love calls for a study of the love passage recorded in 1 Corinthians 13:1–8.

When a Woman Loves a Man

Although this discussion is directed toward women, let me be the first one to acknowledge that love is a two-way street. No one can argue with the fact that, in an exchange of love, it definitely takes two. To that point, men have equally as much to learn. But since we're in a discussion that is geared for women, let's allow the apostle Paul to speak on the authority of God's Word.

"If I speak with the tongues of men and of angels, but do not have love, I have become a noisy gong or a clanging cymbal. If I have the gift of prophecy, and know all mysteries and all knowledge; and if I have all faith, so as to remove mountains, but do not have love, I am nothing. And if I give all my possessions to feed the poor, and if I surrender my body to be burned, but do not have love, it profits me nothing. Love is patient, love is kind and is not jealous; love does not brag and is not arrogant, does not act unbecomingly; it does not seek its own, is not provoked, does not take into account a wrong suffered, does not rejoice in unrighteousness, but rejoices with the truth; bears all things, believes all things, hopes all things, endures all things. Love never fails; but if there are gifts of prophecy, they will be done away; if there are tongues, they will cease; if there is knowledge, it will be done away."

Paul structured his teaching on love in the following way. In verses 1 through 3, he wrote about the priority of love. In verses 4 through 7, he described the properties of love. And in verse 8, Paul culminated with the permanence of love.

Let me give you some background on what initially motivated him to present this powerful explanation of God's greatest gift to humanity. Paul was aware that the members of the Corinthian church were struggling with some issues. Among some serious faults, one problem in particular involved a flaw in their judgment.

You see, they had become misguided into thinking that the gifts of the Spirit were more important than the fruit of the Spirit. So he brought to their attention that the believers had given the least gift; that is, the gift of tongues, the greatest priority over all.

Most assuredly, it was not that the gifts of the Spirit weren't important because God has a reason for everything He gives us. Rather, in his leadership role, the apostle needed to help the church understand that although the believers had the ability to operate in an array of gifts—the most important thing that every person needs to imitate is God's love.

The Corinthians had been bragging about how effective they were at speaking to God. Paul had to tell them that practicing the love of God toward one another is greater than any words one can say. There is a familiar phrase used to describe his point. We've all heard or said it at one time or another: Actions speak louder than words.

　　　　　　　　　　　　　　When a Woman Loves a Man

So Paul proceeded to pull the covers off of their misguided behavior and thinking, articulating a troubling situation I've observed many times. I have encountered people who claim to speak to God in an unknown language but wouldn't speak to me in English.

If you know someone like that, you need to realize something. They don't understand that what a person says with their mouth doesn't amount to anything if they don't back it up with love. That is the first lesson we all need to learn about love because our primary focus in life should be on showing love to God's people. If we could all just get this one thing right, the world would be a better place. Relationships like the one exposed in my opening story would be nonexistent.

Next, Paul confronted the church about their claim to having the faith and knowledge to solve all mysteries. Once again, they were missing the point. He called them out on this, explaining that it's more important for someone to exercise love than it is for them to boast about what they might know.

His meaning was clear. Having faith is necessary to do good works. But he said that faith without love is useless. The main thing they needed to do was allow the head knowledge they had about God to flow from their head down to their heart. And the same message applies today.

To round off his teaching, the apostle reminded them that

everything else was going to eventually pass away. But when it's all said and done, love will stand the test of time. So what will the wise person take away from this? At the end of the day, showing love is far greater than anything else that one can say, think, or do.

WHAT'S LOVE GOT TO DO WITH IT?

Here's the principle. We can say that we love, but unless there is a genuine demonstration of God's love to go along with that proclamation, then we really don't have anything to support our words. I think that was the point of the autobiography of that great pop artist, Tina Turner. After much pain and anguish, she realized that allowing her husband, Ike, to physically harm her was not a sign of showing him love. She had misguidedly thought that was the way he *needed* her to love him.

If you saw the movie about her life, her friends came to her and said, "What's wrong with you, girl?" Ms. Turner responded in so many words, "Well, he's having problems ... and I love him." Now, most people recognize that her reaction involved a good deal of irrational thinking. You don't allow someone to misuse you simply because you think that's the way to love that person. The moral of this story is: Enduring physical and mental violence has nothing to do with love.

After she saw the light, Ms. Turner wrote about her motivation through the lyrics of a song. She discovered that accepting his abuse didn't express her love for him; rather, it exposed her own self-hatred. Consequently, in response to her epiphany she came up with a song that hit the top of the charts, "What's Love Got to Do with It?"

We all have to get this: At the end of the day, the talk and the walk have to match. If there is any inconsistency between what you say and how you love, then you are not espousing true love. Like the apostle stated, it won't stand the test of time.

The Greatest Love

Of course, God Himself offered us the greatest demonstration of love. As Scripture informs us,

> "God so loved the world, that He gave His only begotten Son, that whoever believes in Him shall not perish, but have eternal life." (John 3:16)

The lesson He taught us about love is priceless. If God hadn't given up His Son for us, we would be eternally lost. But since He gave the greatest sacrifice, it is a validation of His love. Now it is the believer's privilege to spend eternity with Him, and for that gift we should embrace God with open arms.

As if that were not enough, the God who controls the universe didn't stop there. He wanted us to be prepared for life on this earth so He equipped us with the ability to not only relate to His love, but to actually imitate it. We know that God has placed His Spirit of love inside each of us for Scripture tells us, "The love of God has been poured out within our hearts through the Holy Spirit who was given to us" (Romans 5:5). So now we have the ability to relate to His love and actually imitate it. And that is exactly what He expects us to do.

Within the context of the marriage relationship, there is a similarity to the illustration of love highlighted in John 3:16. God's expression of love was tangible. He *gave* His Son. When a woman loves a man, there are certain visible, outward signs of her love. In other words, her love must be tangible—she has to give of herself sacrificially as well. Through very visible, touchable means, she shows her husband how much she cares for him. The best way to do this is to follow God's command and the example of Jesus Christ.

FORMULA FOR A LOVING AND CARING WIFE

We've come to the final note in the symphony of love that is expressed through God's Word. When a woman loves a man, she cares for him. At first glance, you might think that this is no big deal. Showing someone that you care couldn't possibly be that difficult. Right? Well, maybe on the surface it sounds easy, but when two married people are confronted with the challenges of sharing life together, it's not always a bed of roses. Loving another human being becomes quite a different story.

So how does she make this work? The first thing to note is that the entire presupposition of a woman caring for a man and being a virtuous woman is predicated on her link and her hookup to the living God.

When a woman's relationship with the Lord is strong and secure, her love flows in this order:

her connection to God →
    influences her character →
        affects her conduct toward her husband and others

It is a virtuous woman's connection to God that gives her the desire to care for her husband. So when a woman loves a man, she puts her heart and soul into caring for him, and nothing pleases her more, because she knows that she is pleasing God. Coming from this special place inside of her, her ability to care begins with the context of her character. Accordingly, her character informs her conduct until altogether she becomes the kind of wife described in Proverbs 31.

These are the elements that make her a virtuous woman. Let me point out that the word "virtuous" is an adjective that describes the woman King Solomon was writing about. Furthermore, the King James Version uses the word "woman" but the modern translations use the word "wife."

The Hebrew word is *ish-shah* and it is used throughout the book of Genesis to describe the woman. For instance, Genesis 2:23, when Adam said, "She shall be called *Woman* because she was taken out of Man," he used the word *ish-shah*.

This is very significant because a virtuous woman has to do with her different roles and relationships. She can be a daughter, a mother, an aunt, or a businesswoman. In other words, it has to do with who she is as a woman. She is full of virtue before she becomes a wife.

A Grim Reality

For those who are contemplating marriage, there is something I must note here because it is germane to this discussion. Do not be deceived. If a woman is not a virtuous woman before she gets married, she won't be a virtuous woman after she gets married. Even while she is single, it's very possible to evaluate her character. In terms of her conduct and personality, whatever she does now, she will do later.

For instance, before she becomes a wife, if she doesn't keep a clean house, it will be the same afterward. If she doesn't take care of herself properly, then her children's hair and clothing will be unkempt as well. If she is not considerate of her financial situation, she won't be a good steward of finances after marriage. If she is not loyal to anyone before marriage, she won't be loyal after.

In other words, if a woman is going to be a virtuous wife she must first be a virtuous woman. If she does not care now, she won't care then.

Here is the reason. A woman's approach to being a wife will be reflected in her character. She already possessed godly character before she entered the marriage relationship. On the other hand, if her character doesn't reflect that of a virtuous woman, it hasn't been influenced by the Lord. Then the care she provides won't be genuine and it won't last very long.

That's why I tell engaged couples all the time that they'd better be observant. I say look at what you've got right now because that's probably the best it's going to get. Now there could be divine intervention; I'm not ruling out the miraculous. But they don't like to hear my warning because it sounds like I'm putting a sour note on their marriage. I believe it's only fair to caution them that five years from now when the honeymoon is over they might look at each other and say, "You've changed."

In most cases, the woman didn't change (and neither did the man, for that matter). Then why does she seem to be so different? Because the husband-to-be *thought* he was getting that young lady who sat across from him at the restaurant and agreed with everything he said. The one who liked everything he wore and didn't mind going wherever he wanted to go before they got married.

The real deal is, unless she has a strong relationship with God and her character and conduct reflect the traits of a virtuous woman—that wasn't the real woman. She was camouflaged. Then after signing on the dotted line, she took off her disguise. Once the honeymoon is over, reality sets in and her true personality will be revealed.

All I'm trying to tell you is, look beyond what you see because that may only be pretty wrapping paper over an empty box. You need to be very observant and rely on God to give you direction and wisdom. What you see is what you get—no more, no less.

Be Fruitful

Emanating from the life of a virtuous wife, an observer will readily see the fruit of the Spirit: love, joy, peace, longsuffering, kindness, goodness, faithfulness, gentleness, and self-control (Galatians 5:22–23). On the other hand, if God's traits are not in evidence, something very different will surface. For example, people can detect the difference between genuine kindness and gentleness and some phony behavior disguised as these traits. If a woman doesn't practice self-control, it won't take long for her behavior to give her away.

The characteristics of a virtuous wife are expressed through the attitude that she takes toward her husband. He will see the fruit of the Spirit in her character and conduct in the following three ways. Study these guidelines to see if you recognize yourself. An excellent wife's demeanor will be: regimented, rigorous, and resourceful.

Regimented. Scripture tells us that love is patient and kind (1 Corinthians 13:4). When a woman loves a man, she will be systematic in the loving care that she gives her husband. As a result, her love is not predicated on the behavior of the man but on the character of the woman. This is true even when there is "trouble in paradise." She doesn't keep track of who's right and who's wrong; instead she continues to express her kindness and unconditional love for him.

For instance, a woman who cooks breakfast for her husband every morning will do it consistently. It doesn't depend on whether there is a dispute going on or because he didn't do what she wanted him to. She is not easily provoked and simply won't stop treating him well over a disagreement. Instead, she will serve him patiently and trust God to rectify every unfair thing she has to tolerate.

Some of the synonyms for "regimented" are: "orderly," "controlled," "restrained," and "regulated." When directed toward her, all of these terms speak to the virtuous wife's disciplined behavior. She won't flare up in jealous fits and act in unbecoming ways because that doesn't fit in her character. Always putting his needs first, she is not selfish and self-centered. There is no "me first" attitude about her.

Furthermore, a woman's sense of order will dictate how well she deals with authority. But when a woman is not committed to a strong relationship with God, her attitude toward authority is typically disrespectful. Have you ever wondered why some people seem to say "Black" if someone else says "White"? There is nothing wrong with having a different opinion. I'm not talking about that. I'm referring to a person who consistently shows a disregard for anything or anyone who represents authority—including her husband.

Rigorous. Scripture also tells us that love bears all things, believes all things, hopes all things, and endures all things (1 Corinthians 13:7). A woman who possesses godly character can draw from her strength and ability to overcome difficulty. Some of the synonyms for the term "rigorous" are: "thorough," "painstaking," "precise," "meticulous," and "careful." So when a woman loves a man, she will take a rigorous approach to whatever challenge confronts her. The character within her is so strong that it always overcomes the adversity without.

Now some may say that it's unrealistic to put this kind of demand on a woman, and it's just like me to suggest something like this. But such a woman does exist. Recall my example of Ruth, a woman who cherished, covered, and cared for her man. I have to go back and pick up Ruth's story because she is such a rich illustration of a virtuous woman. In fact, listen to how Boaz praised her:

"And he said, Blessed be thou of the Lord, my daughter: for thou hast shewed more kindness in the latter end than at the begin-

When a Woman Loves a Man

ning, inasmuch as thou followedst not young men, whether poor or rich. And now, my daughter, fear not; I will do to thee all that thou requirest: for all the city of my people doth know that thou art a virtuous woman." (Ruth 3:10–11 KJV)

Boaz was very enamored with Ruth and had some admirable things to say about her. He appeared to be quite impressed as he talked about the kindness she had shown him. The word "kindness" also means "goodness." The key word to note here is "good." The woman was good. She held intrinsic value that led to extrinsic action, which meant that she was good. Boaz summed up his assessment of Ruth by calling her "a virtuous woman."

There is a touching and profound end to her story. Ruth received a great reward for her honorable actions as a virtuous woman. Boaz agreed to be her kinsman-redeemer.

Her blessing came as a result of her godly character. She took a rigorous and regimented approach to achieve her goal and was not deterred by any of the things she had to overcome. Putting everything else aside, Ruth demonstrated a high level of dedication. It didn't matter to her that she was different from the other women. Ruth wasn't willing to allow any obstacles to dictate what she could accomplish.

When a woman loves a man, she is in the relationship for the long haul. Her dedication will not be predicated on other people's opinions, life circumstances, or her own ambitions. Her marriage will be long lasting because she will remain faithful to the end. As Scripture puts it, her love will never fail.

Resourceful. What is it that brings a woman to her virtuous state? It is the fear, or reverence, of the Lord. What is it that has developed her character so that she cares and gives her all to her husband? It is her relationship with God. Through the light of God's Word, she will know that she's been given the greatest resource that exists. Furthermore, she will faithfully rely on His direction.

Let me illustrate this for you. My wife and I took the grandchildren to Navy Pier, and we had a good time. If you know how grandkids are, they want this and they want that. It's probably best to just say you don't have any money. That way you can buy what you want them to have instead of everything that they want—which is everything.

It was getting dark and we were ready to leave. Then they wanted the toys that glow in the dark. My grandson said, "Papa, can we get some of those glow things?" We're talking $6 a pop and we had five kids with us. Of course, my wife wanted one too. And since they were all glowing, I didn't want to be left out. I had to get me one. I left there $42 lighter.

On our way home, the toys were glowing in the dark and everybody was happy. All of a sudden, Little J said, "These things are dying." I said, "Dying?" Well, they were getting dim. They weren't

When a Woman Loves a Man

as bright as they were. Then I had a surprise for them. I said, "Don't worry. I can fix that." He said, "You can fix it, Papa?" You see, because I'm his granddad, I can fix everything.

But I had something over them. I could read and they couldn't. The tag stated that after a while the toys will get dim. The way to get it to light up again is to wrap it around a light source and expose it to light. So when we got home that's what I did. I wrapped them around a light bulb and exposed them to light.

My grandson said, "Look, they're starting to glow again!"

This is my second time around, so I take every opportunity to be with him and to teach him about the things of God. And he understands more than people would think.

I said, "You know what? This is just like Christians." He said, "What do you mean, Papa?" I said, "You see, we have a light because we've been born again and this light is in us. It's the light of Christ. Now that light makes us do what we're supposed to do. But sometimes when we're not in fellowship (by that I mean being with Him and wrapped around Him), what happens is our light gets dim and pretty soon if we don't wrap ourselves around the Light, our light will go totally dark."

I went on to explain, "That's a believer—still saved but the light has grown dim. What we have to do in order to get our light back to where it needs to be is wrap ourselves around Jesus because He's the Source of our light.

Then he said something very profound, "Oh, maybe that's what's going on in my family." That was very perceptive.

And so what happens when a woman loves a man? She's able to pull it off because she's wrapped around the true Source of Light. The virtuous woman that Solomon described is set forth as a model. She is costly and rare. Every woman does not reflect this kind of virtue. It's not every woman whom you will encounter. I wish that it were. It is the one who stands head and shoulders above other individuals; she will be called a virtuous woman because of her relationship with God, her godly character, and her godly conduct.

She knows how to rely on her greatest resource; the light that guides her way is her fellowship, her communion with God. She has a steady supply of grace that reinforces her so that the care and the conduct that radiates from her life is just as strong as the light from which it gets its source.

THE PRICE IS RIGHT?

When King Solomon described the character of the ideal woman, he wrote that her worth is far above rubies (Proverbs 31:10). Why did he use rubies as a comparison to her value? Why didn't he just use gold or silver? Why not diamonds? At the time, gold was the most precious commodity. As a medium of exchange, it was used to buy goods. He could have compared her to gold.

The virtuous woman's value is far above anything that is

common. When you think about it, what do you do with precious stones? You put them on display for the world to see. In the same way, God wants to put you, His precious virtuous woman, on exhibition so that you can model His ideal traits. He wants others to see how they too will be blessed when they follow His pattern. Women, make sure you are a true model and not a mannequin. You are to strut down the runway displaying God's creation of a godly woman. Don't let the world dress you in their ideas of a good woman.

If you're struggling with what God is doing in your life, know that we all have struggles. At some point He gave you a promise and it doesn't seem like any of it is coming to fruition. You've been waiting and wondering when you are going to reach the desired end that God promised. My message to you is, don't give up on God. He has placed a value on you that is far beyond comparison, and you are more valuable to Him than you could ever imagine.

Let me give you another example. I went to a local grocery store and purchased several items, including some milk, lettuce, franks, a dozen eggs, a bunch of bananas, and a package of rolls. When the cashier rang up my purchases, this is what she told me, "Sir, that will be $236.39." I said, "What did you say?" She repeated it and then she realized that didn't sound right.

I'm thinking, *I know inflation is high, but this is ridiculous.* We both looked up on the screen, and it showed that the price of a twelve-ounce package of rolls was $211.50. Of course, it was a mistake. There was no way I would pay that amount for the rolls, and the manager walked over to correct the price.

But what happened here? The cashier mistakenly placed a higher value on those rolls than it should have been and it had to be changed. Why couldn't she just leave it and say, "Look, if you don't want it, then don't buy it"?

Let me tell you why. The manufacturer put a price on the value of the item and sent it to the retailer. Since the price quoted to me was too high, I had the right to contest it and demand the correct value.

Now, look at this situation in reverse. Is there a similar problem where women are concerned? No. In this case, we've set the value too low. The Manufacturer of the woman has already placed a value on her, and no one has the right to lower that value.

In God's sight, women are to be highly esteemed. After God brought Eve into being, He didn't say, "It is good" like He did when He created Adam. He said that His work was "very" good. God made this distinction to demonstrate that He placed something in the woman that He didn't give to the man. He intensified the extreme value that He added to the woman.

And, no, I am not saying that God values woman more than man. Here is my point. God intensified a particular characteristic of her nature that is not as intense in the man. It's called nurturing.

If you study the word "nurture" the words "good" and "nurture" come from the same root in the Hebrew. So God is saying that women have been given an exceptional tendency to nurture. Therefore, the act of caring that a woman is capable of is something that comes from the way that she was designed.

That's why she has mercy on her children when they've done something wrong. For instance, if little Jimmy neglects to do one of his chores, Mama will let him get away with a warning. But it may not be so easy to convince Daddy to give him a break.

Why is this? Mama's sense of compassion usually overrides her disappointment when it comes to her children. On the other hand, Daddy is pragmatic, and he's basically not a nurturer. All he sees is that the lawn wasn't mowed when it should have been.

THE ART OF CARING

When a person cares for someone, it is shown through tangible ways—things that you can see and touch. The principles of a woman's ability to care are broken down this way. When a woman loves a man, she provides:

Comprehensive care. Her husband doesn't want for anything because she makes sure that whatever he needs will be provided. Her husband is free to do what he needs to support the family and doesn't have to worry about coming home and making his own dinner or cleaning his own house. I know that today many wives also have jobs. But, according to the Bible, the job shouldn't take priority over her God-given priority, which is to manage the household. For a virtuous woman, this is not an issue because she is also a good organizer and has set things in a way so that her outside job should not interfere with her primary job.

Consistent care. When a woman loves a man she faithfully takes care of every need that concerns him. She provides the support that is necessary for him to be the leader of the household. Here is how one man described the situation: The ideal wife is one who sits up with you when you're sick and puts up with you when you're not.

Conditionless care. When a woman loves a man, Scripture says that she will do him good and not evil all the days of her life. Notice what it does not say. The Bible doesn't say all the days of her life—as long as he is the spiritual leader he ought to be. It doesn't say all the days of her life—as long as he provides like he's supposed to provide. Neither does it say all the days of her life—as long as he doesn't make her upset or do anything wrong. No, it says all the days of her life—period. That's it.

You have to understand that this is total care. It is not based on any condition or criteria that she expects of her husband. It's a mind-set based on the character of the woman. The virtuous woman's actions and attitude are unswerving toward the way that she shows concern for her husband. Every deed and action speaks this sentiment, "I don't care; I'm going to care anyway."

Remember that God has made her a helpmate for her husband. When He called her a helper, she was given the same characteristics that He has as our Helper. God's care does not hold conditions, and the care she is to provide is not predicated on conditions.

It's not that this is so easy for her to do; her attitude is simply, "I *have* to do this." Her motivation is driven by her relationship with God. And because of the love she has for the Lord, she is able to do what she needs to do. Her motto remains: *Whatever he needs, I'll provide.*

Stay Connected

Through the bond that you have with God, you learn firsthand how God treats His beloved. You have been given a big task, and in order to accomplish it, take your direction from the Lord. Imitate Him. The mercy and lovingkindness that He shows you, do the same for your mate.

You see, on the road of life, God has put within us a divine navigational system, called the Holy Spirit. When we accepted Jesus Christ, the Holy Spirit took up residence in our lives. He is the One who links us up to the Father.

As we're driving along this journey, we sometimes lose our way. In many situations we're found wondering what we should do because things aren't going right in the dynamics of our relationships. Difficulties arise that are often unavoidable between married couples. Child rearing can be challenging. Engaged couples struggle with compatibility issues. But in every case, all we need to do is push a button called prayer.

The Bible tells us that the Holy Spirit is ever ready to help us overcome every obstacle. Even when we don't know what to pray, this is the assurance we have:

> "The Spirit also helps our weakness; for we do not know how to pray as we should, but the Spirit Himself intercedes for us with groanings too deep for words." (Romans 8:26)

Sometimes our human language is insufficient to express what's going on inside of us. Even though you don't know exactly how to articulate what you want to say, you don't have to worry about it. Just push the button called prayer. The heavenly satellite system monitors you and knows where you are and knows exactly what to do.

So you get on your knees and you speak God's Word back to Him, "Lord, I trust in You with all of my heart. I will not lean to my own understanding. In all my ways I acknowledge You and You promised to direct my path." When the Holy Spirit ascends to the third heaven and the Heavenly Father hears that prayer, He communicates with us by His Spirit. We receive not only the direction but the internal power to triumph over our circumstances.

When a Woman Loves a Man

We are able to exhibit the character of God because of our relationship with Him.

So it really doesn't matter who you're married to or who your intended mate may be. The question is: Are you linked up to God? Have you wrapped your light around His glorious lamp and allowed God to reinforce your character so that you will become what God wants you to become?

Consider what happened on our behalf. Jesus made the ultimate sacrifice. He gave His crown to the Father. Then He gave His deity to humanity. He gave up His heavenly home for an earthly one. Then He gave His life on Calvary. But before that, He gave His back to the whip and His head to a crown of thorns. Then after giving His mother to John and His body to the ground—He arose. And He didn't stop giving even then. He gave the Holy Spirit on the day of Pentecost. He gave us to become the body of Christ. He gave the indwelling and sealing ministry of the Holy Spirit. He gave us spiritual blessings in heavenly places.

And He's still giving. He's at the right hand of the Father making interception for us. He's giving us His prayers. He gave us His presence so that we would never be alone. He gave us His power so when the fullness of Christ is in us, we're able to accomplish our purpose. He just keeps on giving. And one day the Bible says He will give these bodies to immortality and we shall see Him and we shall be as He is.

Having done all this for you, can you not find it in your heart to give back to the Lord the thing that He asks? Follow His pattern and be obedient to His commandments. If you are a woman, be a virtuous one. If you are a wife, be a virtuous one. If you set your heart on showing him a tangible love, I guarantee that you won't be wasting your time. God will crown you queen and see to it that you're treated like one.

Think *about it:*

1. Have you ever taken the time to dissect the love passage of 1 Corinthians? Examine each verse and evaluate how well you measure up to the true meaning of love.

2. Why is it necessary to express a genuine love for someone before you can use your faith to do something good for them?

3. Do you recognize the importance of loving yourself before you can love others?

4. What kinds of sacrifices do you make to show your husband that you not only care for him but you also care about him?

5. Explain to a friend or a daughter that a woman must be full of virtue in all of her roles—even before she becomes a virtuous wife.

When a Woman Loves a Man

Live *by it:*

Dear Heavenly Father, thank You for giving us the greatest gift of Your eternal love. Show your daughters how to emulate Your love in tangible ways when it comes to loving their mates. By Your grace, help them to rely on their most precious resource; that is, the light of Your Word that has the power to keep them ever close to You, in Christ's name. So be it.

Chapter Six

the finishing touch

when a woman loves *a man,* she covers him

I HAVE A COMPELLING question for you: Do you spend time reading the Bible for enrichment and enjoyment? I do hope you have a real appreciation for the Word of God because, believe me, soap operas don't have anything on this superb Book. If you would make a habit of reading it more often, you'd never have to watch another soap opera or reality show. I assure you that the fascinating stories you'll find there are better than anything you can view on a television set.

This next vignette about a married woman is absolutely engrossing. It reinforces what I've posited from the beginning.

There is a marvelous design that was inspired by God for women only. Think of it this way: God is the Master Designer. He tested a concept to see if it met the specifications of His divine blueprint. When He put it on display, He expected it to bend where it was supposed to bend and hold where it was supposed to hold.

This is the way that God intended for the woman to function throughout her lifetime. Furthermore, the ability to serve in the role of a wife places particular emphasis on the woman's design as it highlights the symbiotic interactions between marriage partners. In other words, the way in which God designed the woman gives her an exclusive opportunity to shine in her marriage. She has been given the privilege to be the finishing touch in a relationship that is pleasing to the Lord.

At the same time, the marriage bond was so fearfully and wonderfully engineered by the highly complex Supreme Being—that is, God Almighty. Someone with obvious experience in a marital relationship thoughtfully put it this way: There's only two times when a man doesn't understand a woman. One is before they get married, and the other is after they get married.

I would add that the reverse is also true. There are times when a woman doesn't understand a man before or after they're married either. This is the very reason I implore women to follow God's divine blueprint and allow it to guide them in loving their husbands—God's way.

There has been a recurring theme throughout this book. God assigned the woman and the man totally distinct duties and responsibilities. Moreover, there are some things that a man does that a woman should not want to do. There are some things that a man does that a woman can't do. Conversely, there are some things that a woman can do that a man can't do. In the latter case, the first thing that comes to mind is that a man will certainly never be able to have a baby. I'm very thankful for that revelation.

But just to show you where society can confuse the issues between the two sexes, let me digress for a moment and give you an example. Our church provided a great health fair event for the community. When I took an osteoporosis test, it came to my attention that the health questionnaire was biased against men.

I had a problem with the very first question: Are you pregnant? I answered never. The next question was: Have you or are you going through menopause? I said, yes, male. It didn't take long for me to realize that the questions were directed toward women as though the female species alone suffers from the debilitating disease of osteoporosis.

It makes me wonder how many other ways have we been programmed into misguided thinking that leaves the two genders mystified and at odds with each other. Yet, all is not lost. There is no need to panic because God will show us the way. He's done so in the past, and He's still leading us by His Spirit today.

THE BLANKET COVERING OF LOVE

Once there lived a wise woman by the name of Abigail. What I'm about to share from her story was true about this woman *before* she met her husband, and it was true about her *after* she became his wife—because that's the way God designed her. This is the story of a woman who demonstrated that she knew how to cover her husband's faults.

Her story is told in 1 Samuel, chapter 25. She was married to a man named Nabal. Interestingly enough, the Bible didn't have any trouble identifying him as a fool. There are a number of Hebrew words translated "fool" in the Old Testament, ranging in category from the least type of fool to the greatest.

I won't keep you guessing. The name Nabal means "empty-headed and close-minded." It signifies the worst type of fool anyone could be. The Bible describes the negativity that this kind of person projects as such:

"Let a man meet a bear robbed of her cubs, rather than a fool in his folly." (Proverbs 17:12)

Sounds like someone that no one wants to be around, doesn't it?

But his better half, Abigail, was just the opposite. She was an intelligent woman who knew that her husband was a fool. Not only that, he was a wealthy fool.

As the story goes, King Saul had started hating David; therefore, David was running for his life. Now the barley harvest and the wheat harvest were over, and there was no food to be had in the fields.

David and his men were hungry, so he came up with a plan. The rich man, Nabal, had hundreds of sheep grazing in the forest. Since David had been a shepherd, he knew something about how thieves plot to steal from the herd. To prevent this from happening to Nabal, David and his men surrounded his flock and kept constant watch over them.

Thinking that Nabal would be grateful for his protection, David sent his messengers to greet Nabal and tell him of how David's army had kept his sheep safe in the wilderness. In return, David requested Nabal to show some generosity and send food for him and his men. Without even giving it a second thought, Nabal became belligerent and flatly refused. He even tried to act as though he didn't know who David was.

When David was informed of this ungrateful man's refusal, he became angry and immediately set out to exact revenge. Commanding his men to get ready for battle, he was prepared to destroy Nabal and everything that belonged to him.

Fortunately for Nabal, one of her husband's servants told Abigail what was about to go down. As soon as she found out, Abigail reacted swiftly. She probably thought to herself, *Oh no, he's done it again.* It would have been a costly mistake to turn her back on

Nabal and leave him to his own devices. So without taking precious time to talk it over with him, she gathered together loads of food and set out to meet David and his army.

Knowing that her husband's judgment couldn't be trusted, sure enough, when she encountered David, he told her that Nabal had repaid his kindness with evil. Immediately, she bowed to the ground and pleaded with David, saying,

> "On me alone, my lord, be the blame. And please let your maidservant speak to you, and listen to the words of your maidservant." (1 Samuel 25:24)

Abigail knew that Nabal had once again lived up to his name. So she responded to David in the way that Nabal should have. Using all the skill and diplomacy that she could muster, she had to convince David that he shouldn't harm Nabal and his possessions. Surely Abigail was the covering her husband needed. Without her, he would have definitely been dead meat.

I will be the first to admit that some of us brothers need to understand that sometimes we don't realize what we've got. As a result, brothers need to take heed; because if a man doesn't treasure his good woman, someone else will. If the two ever go their separate ways, there will usually be somebody eagerly waiting to step into his place.

When a Woman Loves a Man

What do we learn from Abigail's story? When a virtuous woman loves a man, she will cover him. This is how Abigail added the finishing touch to her marriage. Here are the elements of how a woman's covering can make a difference in her husband's well-being.

1. Be aware of his character.

To keep her husband from being harmed, Abigail reasoned with David. Listen to what she said to him:

> "Please do not let my lord pay attention to this worthless man, Nabal, for as his name is, so is he. Nabal is his name and folly is with him; but I your maidservant did not see the young men of my lord whom you sent." (1 Samuel 25:25)

Now, recall what I said previously because it definitely applies to Abigail. God built the woman to endure a crash against the wall of adversity. She has the innate ability to bend where she needs to bend and hold where she needs to hold. Clearly, this woman could hold where she ought to hold.

Not only did the Scripture say that Abigail was beautiful in appearance, but she was an intelligent woman who knew how to handle a time of crisis. She made up for his lack of common sense when Nabal was in a serious predicament and he didn't even know it. He had disrespected the next king of Israel. He had no idea who he was going up against. David had killed the giant Goliath. When he was seventeen years old, he grabbed a lion by the beard and killed him. You don't play with someone like that.

But what did God give him because God knew he was stupid? He gave Nabal a wise woman who understood her husband's character and was willing to protect him from his own foolish ways.

Let me pause here for a moment. I want to confess that there are areas where I'm stupid. And I'm so glad that God gave me a wise woman. Fortunately for me, I stopped rebelling against her and started accepting it. Now I realize that I have a blind side and God gave me my wife to cover me in times when I would otherwise act blindly. I can only hope that other brothers would open their eyes and recognize what they have before it's too late.

2. Be willing to correct his mistakes.

To cover for his faults, Abigail gave David the three things that Nabal didn't give him: recognition, respect, and resources.

a. Nabal failed to recognize David's position of authority. Abigail corrected his error in judgment when she fell at David's feet. She sought to support her husband by making up for his poor manners.

b. Nabal didn't give David his due respect. He talked down to

When a Woman Loves a Man

the next king of Israel. Abigail made up for that too by addressing David with the title "my lord," which is the equivalent of saying, "sir" or "master." To diffuse the obvious offense her husband had caused, she showed David honor and respect.

c. Nabal refused to give David some resources that he had actually earned. To make up for his selfish nature, Abigail gathered plenty of resources and took them to David. Her counteraction to Nabal's selfishness brought about a blessing of protection for them from the Lord.

Abigail did everything that she could to make things right with David. Now I know what you're thinking. The Bible says she didn't tell her husband what she was about to do. Would that not be considered a disregard for his authority by going behind her husband's back? In this case, I would say no. She had to act quickly. David was coming after them to kill them. There was no time to try to convince an empty-headed fool that he had to do something quickly.

3. Be committed to him.

When she spoke to David on her husband's behalf, Abigail knew what she was talking about. Her mission was to cover Nabal's faults and protect them both from harm. So she explained the entire situation to David and humbly pleaded her case. Now don't miss this. By her actions, she showed her commitment of loyalty to Nabal. In essence, she was saying this is just how he is.

You see, if you're ever going to be a covering for your husband, you'll have to show your loyalty to him—when it feels good and when it doesn't. You'd better know him. He is not strong enough to guard against his own weaknesses. Get to know his weaknesses because you're going to have to guard them for him. You need to know what he is capable of doing. You've got to know what kind of women he likes. You've got to know what kind of recreation he loves. Show your commitment to him by getting to know your husband.

Take your cue from the example Abigail modeled. I don't know your personal situation and perhaps it isn't quite as bad as hers, but clearly, God gave her to Nabal because he didn't have much sense. She explained to David that she wasn't with Nabal when this occurred. If she had been, things would have turned out differently.

Abigail knew her man and her strength for him. She would have reasoned with him when he turned down David's request. Moreover, she wouldn't have done it out in public. She would have had enough sense to speak with him privately and say something like, "Nabal, may I talk to you for a minute, please? Let me just share something with you."

Then she would have broken down the situation for him: "Now, this man is going to be the next king of Israel. He's hungry,

When a Woman Loves a Man

desperate, and running for his life. He has all those men with him, and if he really wanted to, he could have taken what he wanted. Instead, he showed that he was a man of honor by helping you. Because of him, you didn't lose anything. And more importantly, we'll be able to keep our lives. He means business; he took a slingshot and killed a giant. We don't want to mess with him."

What would have been the effect if she had been given the opportunity to do this? She would have been acting like any virtuous wife should in a tight situation by showing her commitment to him.

Maybe your husband is imperfect enough that you've had to deal with some adverse circumstances. If so, this is your opportunity to show God that you desire to be the finishing touch for your husband. It is your mission to cover for him. You may know that he isn't right, but no one else better talk about him. The reason? He's still your man.

You can admit that he's stupid (and only to God), but no one else can call him that. Your girlfriends can disrespect their men like that. But you should tell them, "Don't let my man's name fall out of your mouth. He's wrong, but he's mine. He's running off, but he's mine. He's not doing what he's supposed to do, but he's mine. And I know that God gave him to me." That's what I call a strong commitment.

Just remember, if you show honor to God by loving the man

that He joined you together with in holy matrimony, God will honor you in ways that you probably can't even imagine right now. But you have to know that it will be a labor of love that grows from an understanding of why you need to be committed to your husband—even if it seems like a hard thing to do.

Once again, Scripture provides the answer:

"Above all, keep fervent in your love for one another, because love covers a multitude of sins." (1 Peter 4:8)

That labor of love indicates a work in progress. It will mean that you continue to forgive him, even if he makes the same old tired mistake many times over. Rather than stirring up past grievances and constantly reminding him that he messed up "again," take the approach God uses with us. When it comes to your personal faults, God is faithful to forgive your every sin. Now put yourself in your mate's shoes. Don't give up on him. He needs your continual forgiveness so that the two of you can move forward.

Abigail took this principle to another level. She kept God's commandment and covered her husband's sin by making his sin, her sin. Now can you get this, ladies? Check out the words of a virtuous wife. Although she had done nothing wrong, she pleaded her case with David, saying, "Please forgive the transgression of your maidservant" (verse 28).

Now, wait just a minute. Abigail claimed responsibility for her husband's transgression. She said to David, if she had been present it wouldn't have been a problem. In other words, it was her fault because she should have been there to avoid the potentially costly and embarrassing mistake her husband made. Why would she identify with his sin? She did so because she was aware of one essential fact. She knew that whenever God joins two people together in marriage, the two become one. Her identity was lost in her husband's and she knew it.

Consequently, her actions are a reflection of what is true for all married women. Every wife must reach this same conclusion and make a declaration such as this: "I'm a part of him. Nothing he does by himself is in isolation of our relationship. Everything he says, every place he goes, everybody he comes in contact with—it all affects me.

"If he's careless and he loses his money, that's my money too. If he's irresponsible and he wrecks his car, that's my car too. If he's reckless and loses his reputation, I lose mine too. I'm in this thing with him even though I didn't do anything wrong. I suffer the consequences of what the one I'm hooked up with does. And most of the time I pay a much higher emotional expense than anybody could ever imagine."

I know that it's a challenge, but can you trust God to handle the intricate details of God's design for you? He has equipped you to do it, and Abigail proved it when she was put on display. She identified with his sin and made it her own. She could do it because she followed the divine design of a virtuous wife. As a result, she changed the outcome of what could have been a devastating and deadly event. And she was rewarded greatly for her efforts. Listen to what David says in response to her willingness to do what was right in God's eyes:

"Nevertheless, as the Lord God of Israel lives, who has restrained me from harming you, unless you had come quickly to meet me, surely there would not have been left to Nabal until the morning light as much as one male." (1 Samuel 25:34)

Because of the way that she handled herself, Abigail not only received his respect, she got David's attention too. David informed her that she had restrained him from hurting her and so many others. This woman succeeded in covering her husband's mistakes and rectifying his wrongdoing. She is an example of what God expects from every wife.

Now, you may say, "But you don't know what I'm dealing with. I'm in a mess because of him." Well, you've heard how dire Abigail's situation was; it could have been fatal. Yet, without hesitation, she rose to the occasion. She didn't stop to think about all the times her husband had caused her pain and embarrassment. She simply

When a Woman Loves a Man

decided to overlook all of that and react in such a way that would alleviate the danger facing their lives at that moment. Her commitment to him wouldn't allow her to just sit back and allow his foolish behavior to destroy everything they had.

And, guess what? God is looking for that level of commitment from you too, wife. He wants to put you on display and show you off as one of His prized models of a virtuous wife. Whether you realize it or not, He had Abigail's back and He has yours too. So don't dismay. Follow the trail of love that the Lord has placed in your heart because, I promise you, it will not lead you astray.

In fact, here is the most important point of all. The basis of Abigail's actions was spiritual. God caused her to not only be aware of her husband's shortcomings; she also knew how to address David. No doubt she may have heard of him, but he was nevertheless a complete stranger to her.

How do I know? Prior to this incident, the Bible gave no indication that she ever even had a conversation with David. This tells me that God was leading her because she demonstrated wisdom and confidence in how to handle the situation. And we all know that wisdom comes from God.

Let me also interject my observations about relationships between women and men. Women more so than men are able to evaluate an individual and generally form an accurate assessment. Moreover, they can usually do so in a relatively short period of time. Now, of course, sometimes they are wrong because no one is perfect. But most of the time, what they conclude is true.

For example, a woman can discern when individuals are suspect and shady—both men and women. If a wife warns her husband to stay away from someone, he'd do best to listen to her. Part of God's design of the woman is an inborn ability that is commonly called woman's intuition, and it is very real.

That's the kind of instinct Abigail demonstrated; she determined that David was a godly man. And so the basis of her conversation with him centered on God and David's devotion to Him. In verse 26, she related to David by saying it was by the providence of God that he didn't harm anyone. In other words, God set it up.

In verse 27, she talked about the provision of God, bringing his attention to the gifts that she brought as a blessing to David and his men. Who gives blessings? All blessings come from God. What is she saying? "God gave this to us so we can give it to you. Through us, God is providing for you."

Then in the verse that followed, she asked for his pardon. Now who talks about pardoning? God has the ultimate authority to forgive. Well, who talks about forgiveness more than anybody else in the Bible? David. He could definitely connect with how she related to him.

Finally, in the next two verses, this wise woman reminded him that he was being prospered by God. With the Lord fighting his

When a Woman Loves a Man

battles, there was no need to take matters into his own hands. David couldn't argue with her because her meaning was indisputable: "Why would you want to do this?"

All in all, Abigail was a virtuous wife who covered her husband's faults. And so many men have wives and fiancées like her. But the real tragedy is, we're Nabals; we don't listen to our women.

MISSION ACCOMPLISHED

Eventually, Abigail opened Nabal's eyes to the whole situation. After she returned from saving their lives, the Bible says he was having a feast and he was very drunk (verse 36). We should all know that there's only one thing worse than a fool and that is a drunken fool.

Being the prudent wife that she was, Abigail used good judgment and waited until the next morning to tell her husband what she had done. Listen to the account: "But in the morning, when the wine had gone out of Nabal, his wife told him these things, and his heart died within him so that he became as a stone" (verse 37).

Generally speaking, a man who's sobering up from a hangover doesn't want to talk much. That way she could take a calm approach and wouldn't even have to raise her voice. Notice his response because it represents something significant. Even though he was a fool, he couldn't help but realize that God had given him a wife who was such a blessing.

After she told him what went down, his heart died within him and he became like a stone. That means he was scared stiff. Some may say he was sweating bullets. But I know he had to be thinking, *Man, I almost blew it. I know I've done some foolish things in my lifetime, but that's got to be the most foolish thing I've ever done.* With a woman like Abigail, any man would have been foolish and crazy to let her go.

Why do I think this is such a great story? Let me tell you why because it doesn't end there. Overall, one gets the impression that God wasn't happy with Nabal's evil behavior. He had disrespected God's chosen one big time. Verse 38 reports that ten days later Nabal died. When David heard the news, guess what happened after the funeral? There was a knock at Abigail's door. Still wearing her black mourning veil, she went to see who it was. There stood messengers sent by David, asking her to be his wife. This was her response to his request,

> "She arose and bowed with her face to the ground and said, 'Behold, your maidservant is a maid to wash the feet of my lord's servants.' Then Abigail quickly arose, and rode on a donkey, with her five maidens who attended her; and she followed the messengers of David and became his wife." (1 Samuel 25:41–42)

Abigail married David. She may have been grieving, but she was also thinking, *This is a good deal.* Her deceased husband had left her a rich woman. Now she would become the wife of the rich and powerful king who would value her counsel.

When Abigail looked back and considered everything that had happened, she must have been thoroughly convinced that the Lord was in control throughout the entire experience. Now, that's a powerful story.

HOPE AGAINST HOPE

Here is the principle. God has given woman the innate ability to be an umbrella of protection and a channel of blessing to man. It's the principle found in 1 Corinthians 7:13–16, which describes the situation where the wife is saved and the husband is not. This passage says that if the man wants to stay, don't kick him to the curb because the unbelieving husband is sanctified by the wife.

What does that mean? If your husband is unsaved and he wants to stay with you, let him stay. There is hope because the blessings of God are coming on you, and God will use you as a channel through which to bless your husband. If you are experiencing financial difficulties and you let him stay, then God will bless you and the lights will stay on for him because God wants the electricity to remain on for you. He won't lose his job even if it's in jeopardy because God wants you to be prosperous, and so He'll let him keep his job. He'll maintain his health because God wants him to be a blessing to you. And so it is that the two of you will bless each other.

Do you get what I'm saying? If he leaves, he will forfeit the umbrella of God's protection. As a result, he will be delivered into Satan's hands. The Enemy of God can do anything he wants to with him because that man is no longer under your shelter and channel of blessings.

But if he comes back to you, God will begin to remedy your marriage for one reason only. It won't be based on what he does because he's like Nabal; it will be due to the fact that you've committed yourself to him. You are fulfilling the design for which you have been created; you are being an *ezer* for your husband.

Think about it this way. We all need help to navigate through life's challenges. God intentionally designed the process so that no one can do it alone. That is why He is the Big Ezer—our Helper. If you rightfully recognize how much you need God's help, so it is with your husband. He needs the help of the one God assigned to him—his little ezer—to help him through life. For the extent of this journey you are his covering, just as God is your covering. That's exactly what's going on.

When a Woman Loves a Man

THE BLESSINGS OF GOD ARE FAR REACHING

There was another woman in the Old Testament who followed God's divine design. And God put her life on display for all to observe. By today's standards, because of her past life she would have been called a hoochie, a skeezer, a hood rat, a trick, or some other term to identify her as a prostitute. But God used her in a powerful way and showed the world that what you do is not necessarily who you are in His eyes.

Her story is found in the book of Joshua, chapter 2. Listen to this account:

"Then Joshua the son of Nun sent two men as spies secretly from Shittim, saying, 'Go, view the land, especially Jericho.' So they went and came into the house of a harlot whose name was Rahab, and lodged there. It was told the king of Jericho, saying, 'Behold, men from the sons of Israel have come here tonight to search out the land.' And the king of Jericho sent word to Rahab, saying, 'Bring out the men who have come to you, who have entered your house, for they have come to search out all the land.' But the woman had taken the two men and hidden them, and she said, 'Yes, the men came to me, but I did not know where they were from. It came about when it was time to shut the gate at dark, that the men went out; I do not know where the men went. Pursue them quickly, for you will overtake them.' But she had brought them up to the roof and hidden them in the stalks of flax which she had laid in order on the roof." (Joshua 2:1–6)

The woman in this story is referred to as a harlot; consequently, she had a bad reputation. Her name was Rahab, and, actually, she had two strikes against her. Not only was she a woman of ill repute, she was also a Gentile.

So what was going on here? Joshua, the leader of God's people, sent two spies into the city of Jericho to check out the land. Old Joshua was smart. You may recall that previously Moses had sent out twelve spies to survey the land, one from every tribe. They were to scout out the territory before the Israelites entered. But ten of them came back with a bad report. This same Joshua was one of the two who returned talking in faith. Now that he was in charge, he decided he would only send two men.

When the two spies went into the city, they found their way to Rahab's house. She recognized them as God's people. Remembering the stories about what God did to Pharaoh and his army, she soon became aware that God was going to do the same thing to her people. So this is what she said to the men: "When we heard it, our hearts melted and no courage remained in any man any longer because of you; for the Lord your God, He is God in heaven above and on earth beneath" (Joshua 2:11).

This was a powerful declaration coming from someone who typically would not acknowledge God. Her words acknowledged that she believed the God of Israel was more than able to give His people the land. Because of her faith, she took courage in her convictions. Therefore, she defied her king and hid the spies, being fully convinced that God was mightier than an army of mere men.

Furthermore, this woman was no fool. In exchange for her protection, she asked the men to spare her entire family. This is what she said: "Now therefore, please swear to me by the Lord, since I have dealt kindly with you, that you also will deal kindly with my father's household, and give me a pledge of truth" (verse 12). They agreed.

For her act of faith, a woman with a once questionable character gained an honorable mention in the Word of God.

You may wonder what made her so special. Well, God designed her and He put her on display. She was single, without a ghost of a chance of getting a husband. As a prostitute, she wasn't accepted in respectable circles. But none of that stopped her from taking a calculated risk and covering for God's people. As a result, God honored what she did for Him.

Before Joshua's army came to take over, Rahab was told to make sure her whole family was inside her house. The promise specified that everybody who was in her house would be saved. If any of her family members living in other parts of the city expected to be saved, they had better come to her house; otherwise, they would be destroyed along with the rest of the city.

Scripture went on to say that Rahab hung the red cord the men had given her in the window. When God's army returned, everyone in her house was spared. Now, how did those people get saved? Was it because they hid the spies? Was it because they believed God? No. The blessing of God was on Rahab's house, and everyone inside was saved because she became an ezer for that house.

Isn't that the principle? Rahab became a channel, a conduit of blessing. Because of her faith and willingness to cover for God's people, she and everybody in her household were preserved. That is the promise of God. The blessing of God was on Rahab's house and everybody else in the city was destroyed.

Then something very interesting happened. After the battle was over, one of the two men that she hid was a brother by the name of Salmon. He was a man of God who recognized Rahab as a woman of faith. He understood that a woman's place was to provide a covering for her man and she had already done that for him. Guess what? Salmon and Rahab were married.

At one time she had been living a scandalous life. But she fit the design of God nonetheless. God tested her faith when she was put on display. He wanted to show all women what He can do when they get into agreement with Him.

But that's not the end of the story; the Bible tells us in Matthew 1:5 that Salmon and Rahab had a son and the son's name was Boaz.

When a Woman Loves a Man

We've already covered his story. Boaz hooked up with a woman by the name of Ruth and they had a son. His name was Obed. And Obed hooked up with a woman and he had a son whose name was Jesse. And Jesse had eight sons, the last of which was David. David then became king of Israel and part of the genealogy of Jesus Christ.

Rahab was privileged to join the lineage of Christ because God displayed her as an exemplary model. Believe it or not, some of the women in this century think that He can't do what He did four thousand years ago. He used a woman who would typically not appear in a Jewish genealogy—never a Gentile woman, let alone one who was a harlot. And this is not just any genealogy; it is the genealogy of the Lord Jesus Christ. He wants every woman to know that fulfilling the divine design will bless her and cause her to be a channel of blessing.

KNOW WHO YOU ARE

Did you notice what happened in Rahab's life? She became a channel of blessing for herself and her entire family. She demonstrated the kind of woman God designed for a man. That display enabled her to marry a man who was attracted to her faithfulness to God.

But that's not the end of the story because when you fast-forward through the pages of Scripture (Matthew 1:3–5), her name is prominently recorded. God used her for a model that others could emulate. He held up a woman who lived thousands of years ago to provide a contemporary, relevant, practical example to the women of the twenty-first century—and beyond. What an awesome God we serve.

If you are feeling misused and unappreciated, know that God has not forgotten you. This is His Word to you:

"His anger is but for a moment, His favor is for a lifetime; weeping may last for the night, but a shout of joy comes in the morning." (Psalm 30:5)

Sometimes in the middle of the night, think about who you are as a woman and the wife God has made you. He called you an ezer, giving you a name that He's only given to Himself, not even to another man. As your husband's helper, you have the unique ability to be a channel of blessing. In fact, you are an exclusive blessing that God gave to a man. You're going to wake up shouting. Your neighbors are going to think somebody is after you because you're going to shout for joy when you find out what God has given to you.

On that morning when you arise, you will find a new and improved mate right before your very eyes. The change in him began taking effect the moment you set your mind to trust God and follow His design for you. But the time will fully come when you will see the change and rejoice in the Lord for the marvelous way He has blessed your marriage. So, my sister, be encouraged.

God is saying to women, all you have to do is know how I designed you. And whenever you crash against the wall of adversity, bend where I made you to bend, hold where I made you to hold. I will then use you as a channel of blessing. I will bless you. I will bless others.

God will put you on display and allow you to be the finishing touch in your relationship. He will show you how to complement your husband in complete submission to him. He will teach you how to cherish and cover him with loving care. He will prosper you and give you peace so that everybody will know that you stayed in the will of God and modeled His design. Then, in the fullness of God's timing, He will give you whatever you desire—according to His will.

Think *about it:*

1. Do you understand why God would encourage a wife to remain by her husband's side even when the man is out of fellowship with Him?
2. Besides a woman's ability to bear children, what are some of the other abilities that God gave exclusively to women?
3. In your own words, explain the principle of a woman jointly taking on her husband's sin.

4. Why does God put significance on this unselfish attitude and behavior?
5. How does a wife's covering of her husband work in practical ways?

Live by it:

Heavenly Father, thank You for my precious sisters in Christ Jesus. Thank You for revealing to them the message of transformation that You want to take place inside their hearts. Show them how to follow Your design from this day forward. Teach Your daughters how to cover for the men You have given them, in Christ's name. So be it.

Conclusion

WHAT IS MORE important to a person's well-being than affirmation and respect? I would wager that the answer is simply— nothing. What does this mean for a loving wife? Her ultimate respect is communicated when she pays attention to and follows her husband's headship.

I realize that God's principles are sometimes difficult to embrace because we have been programmed by society to accept a lower standard. Yet and still, there are women today who exemplify God's divine design. And that is my point. If they can do it, so can others. In fact, some very wise women have learned valuable lessons about supporting their husband's ability to lead. They have devoted their time and efforts to encouraging their mates in the area of personal development.

Just in case there are any lingering doubts about this truth, I will conclude the study of *When a Woman Loves a Man* by using a contemporary model of God's design and display. God is pleased with deeds such as the following and wants to exhibit them for others to observe.

There is a godly woman in my congregation who does an excellent job of esteeming her husband according to the principles that the virtuous woman taught us. I believe it is appropriate to tell this story here because it so effectively sums up the argument I have put forth in this book.

Some time ago, this particular woman wanted to come to worship with us when we were called South Shore Baptist Church. She began visiting our prayer meetings and thoroughly enjoyed herself. After attending several times, she was certain that God would have her and her husband become members of our church.

Shortly thereafter, her husband came to speak with me. He shared with me some things that he had in mind in terms of a church home. He also informed me that he wasn't persuaded that South Shore was the place for them.

That was fine. I understand that church membership is a big decision and each family must determine where they can best accomplish God's purposes. However, his wife was thoroughly convinced that South Shore was the place they needed to be.

At the next prayer meeting, she explained to me: "Pastor, I won't be returning to South Shore. My husband has decided that we are going to join another church. I really believe that this is where God wants us, but I'm going to respect and support my husband. I'm going to follow his leadership. Would you please agree with me in prayer? I'm asking God to give my husband wisdom to

When a Woman Loves a Man

lead and that He would give me grace to follow."

I thought to myself, *Wow! What an excellent attitude.* I knew that God was pleased with the behavior she was demonstrating. So, after we prayed, I asked permission to use her as a sermon illustration and she consented.

Now, what did this godly woman mean by asking God to give her "the grace to follow"? She asked God to help her keep her mouth shut. She wanted to cheerfully cooperate with the decision her husband had made. Although she had already expressed her preference and he had decided to follow another course, she was willing to stand by his decision. Her actions proved that, when a woman loves a man, in good faith she will support his choices.

As it turned out, the church that her husband had chosen was not what he expected after all. They weren't satisfied and didn't stay there very long.

Because she was fully prepared to fulfill God's directive, this wise woman had more choices confronting her. She could have said, "I told you so! We've gone all the way 'round the mulberry bush, only to end up right back at South Shore. That's where I *told you* we should be in the first place . . . " Yet, she didn't give in to that temptation. Instead, she lovingly followed him here.

There may be some women who will say that the way in which she handled the situation was a vain exercise. She should have disagreed with his decision and dismissed him as just being stubborn.

On the contrary. When a wife loves her husband in the way that God intends her to, it is about appreciating his masculinity and not challenging his decisions.

You see, wife, once you can appreciate the fact that God created men with a need and desire to lead, then you will accept the fact that sometimes you will "go 'round the mulberry bush" with your husband. In reality, what you are actually doing is giving him the opportunity to operate in his leadership position and acknowledge the One who leads him.

Moreover, you will know that the conduct you display is virtuous when you respond with a gentle spirit—one that does not oppose or react negatively. You will know that you are a woman of virtue when you respond with a quiet spirit—one that does not worry or become anxious. At the end of the day, it is very likely that you will "win" your husband over. And, as future situations arise, he will be more inclined to listen to and consider your ideas and suggestions with greater concern.

The bottom line is, if you want to live in wisdom with your husband, you will show him that you understand the way he is made and make allowances for the qualities God instilled in him.

One final thought, let me ask you this: Would you expect a fish to live out of water? Would you try to tell a bird not to fly? Let your man be the man. Support him. Encourage him to embrace his tendency and desire to lead. Help him to cultivate and refine

When a Woman Loves a Man

his decision-making skills. Make useful suggestions to him and present him with the advantages and disadvantages of the possible choices before him. In so many words, give him the kind of love that he can feel in all aspects of your relationship.

When you show him your love in tangible ways, God will see to it that, in due time, your husband will respond accordingly. The Word of God is truth, and it is forever settled in heaven. In other words, God won't change His rules. Incorporate the principle of Galatians 6:6–10 into your daily regimen. Scripture promises that if you continue to do your best and do good deeds to others, you will receive a good outcome in life. So don't give up or grow weary in your well-doing. Sow the seeds of a good marriage and God will see to it that good results will come back to you.

This is God's desire for you. Know that you can be the virtuous woman He created you to be. In spite of everything that might try to deter you, it was the God of all grace who placed in you the ability to carry out your role as an excellent wife.

When a woman loves a man, she will always keep the Word of God in her heart, and remember that "a woman who fears the Lord, she shall be praised" (Proverbs 31:30).

My prayer is that our search for the virtuous woman has been fruitful. She has awakened, for we have found her in you. Be continually blessed.

WHEN A MAN LOVES A WOMAN

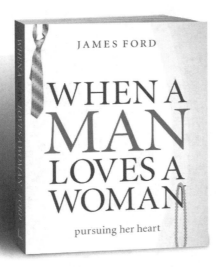

ISBN-13: 978-0-8024-6838-3

In *When a Man Loves a Woman*, Pastor James Ford Jr. uses the story of Jacob and Rachel to teach key principles that will help men win the heart of the woman in their life. This book, along with *When a Woman Loves a Man*, will equip those who are married and those preparing for marriage in pursuing each other's heart.

LEVB
LIFT EVERY VOICE BOOKS

lifteveryvoicebooks.com

SEVEN REASONS WHY GOD CREATED MARRIAGE

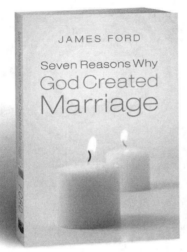

ISBN-13: 978-0-8024-2262-0

In *Seven Reasons Why God Created Marriage*, Pastor James Ford, a seasoned marriage counselor, walks readers through the Bible and shows you seven purposes for which God created marriage. This exploration will reveal timeless truths upon which readers—whether engaged or newly married—can build a solid foundation and strengthen the pillars of their marriage, reaping the benefits God intended along the way.

LIFT EVERY VOICE BOOKS

lifteveryvoicebooks.com